RAMAYANA

by the same author

LOOK WE HAVE COMING TO DOVER!
TIPPOO SULTAN'S INCREDIBLE WHITE-MAN-EATING TIGER-TOY MACHINE!!!

Ramayana

~

A Retelling

DALJIT NAGRA

FABER & FABER

First published in 2013
by Faber and Faber Ltd
Bloomsbury House
74–77 Great Russell Street
London WC1B 3DA

This paperback edition first published in 2014

Typeset by RefineCatch Ltd, Bungay, Suffolk
Printed and bound in England by CPI Group (UK) Ltd, Croydon, CRO 4YY

© Daljit Nagra, 2013

The right of Daljit Nagra to be identified as author of this work
has been asserted in accordance with Section 77 of the Copyright,
Designs and Patents Act 1988

A CIP record for this book is available from the British Library

ISBN 978–0–571–31384–6

FSC
www.fsc.org
MIX
Paper from
responsible sources
FSC® C101712

2 4 6 8 10 9 7 5 3 1

Contents

~

Introduction

~

I CANNOT RECALL a time when I did not know about *Ramayana*. My illiterate grandmother and mother would frequently tell their Punjabi version of the story during the festival of Diwali which celebrates Rama and Sita's homecoming. In my family, I was part of the first generation to be told the story in Britain. This was a story of another place, not my home, so my relationship with it is significantly different to my ancestors'. When I started school and began to learn English, my education removed me further from the rituals of Punjabi language, culture and religion. The *Ramayana* I present now is not the one I was told as a child; instead it is the product of a globalised Westernised writer who lives among many faiths and cultures and who seeks to represent voices from as many villages as possible with the same passion as the version I heard as a child.

The most widely-known storyline of *Ramayana* has been central to my version. Vishnu incarnates himself as Rama in order to vanquish the demon Raavana. When it is time for Rama to become King of Kosala in Ayodhya in northern India, his father is persuaded against this decision and instead Rama is sent into exile followed by his wife, Sita, and his brother, Lakshmana. Whilst in exile, Sita is abducted to Lanka by Raavana who has fallen in love with her. Rama wins the support of a monkey army to help him fight Raavana's troops to win her back.

Ramayana, or 'The Travels of Rama', has a long and complicated history. It probably originated orally in India having been influenced by local folk stories. Most specialists believe that someone known as Valmiki later authored the first written version around 2000 years ago. As a northern Indian poet, Valmiki presents Rama as a warrior hero overcoming a southern demon. In addition to this version, however, many others, in languages other than Sanskrit, later emerged in India. The next major version to be written originated in southern India and its Tamil author, Kamban, presents Raavana more sympathetically. Some subsequent southern versions, take this further by presenting the north as Brahmin, pro-caste and Sanskrit and the south as non-Brahmin, egalitarian and Tamil. Already the written versions were becoming more complex as a result of geographical and cultural interpretations. Beyond India, further variations occurred as *Ramayana* spread across Asia to countries such as Nepal, Tibet, Mongolia, China, Japan, Thailand, Burma, Laos, Cambodia, Malaysia and Indonesia. All of these countries' versions have elements of Valmiki or Kamban's narrative to some degree whilst adding distinctive cultural features of their own. Across Asia *Ramayana* has been represented in a range of artistic forms such as poetry, prose, theatre, film, dance, sculpture and painting, but it remains an oral story for most who know it.

In constructing my *Ramayana,* I tried to incorporate elements from as many versions as possible to enrich the narrative. For example, my account of Rama's causeway to Lanka (in Book Fourth) was influenced by Valmiki and Kamban, but also by the Thai Ramakien version in which the army crosses the bridge in the formation of a dragon; to honour this influence I also incorporated Thai character names into this scene. Another story in Book Fourth involving a father and son buffalo is not prominent in Indian *Ramayanas,* but appears in Thai, Cambodian and Laotian versions. I was also influenced by the image of a Cambodian *Ramayana* mural showing a monkey king breaking out of a cave using a buffalo's head and chose to incorporate this in the scene.

Although it is most widely known as a Buddhist and Hindu text, Jain and Sikh *Ramayanas* also exist. In addition to religious doctrine, regional spiritual philosophies have influenced *Ramayana.* The bhakti tradition which started in southern India before the 10th century AD, for example, emphasizes the intense active attachment to a personal god. This influence can be seen in Kamban's version which focuses on active devotion to Rama in which even recitation of his name can produce miracles. I have tried to respect all of these religious influences in my text including elements from the bhakti tradition.

A story that may be several thousands of years old, that has been persistently altered and that has passed into many languages throughout its extensive history deserves to be honoured by the language in which it is written. *Ramayana* is, in a sense, as much about the power of language and the way it sustains the imagination as it is about the narrative sustaining our interest over time. For these reasons, I have sought to combine the immense historical and cultural wealth of *Ramayana* with an eclectic mix of linguistic influences to highlight the breadth of its appeal. Some readers will be familiar with other *Ramayanas* and I hope that my version will increase their enjoyment of the story. For readers coming to *Ramayana* for the first time, I hope to bring some of the sense of wonder that I felt as a child as well as an appreciation of its long and dynamic tradition.

DALJIT NAGRA

List of Characters

∼

Principal Characters

KING DASARATHA
(dush-RUT-a)
Mighty but elderly King of
Kosala who seeks a male heir.

RAMA
(*RAAM-a – note that 'raam'
means 'peace' in Punjabi*)
Son of King Dasaratha and our
hero.

LAKSHMANA
(LUCK-SHma-na)
Son of King Dasaratha and
Rama's constant companion.

SITA
(*SEE-taa*)
Adopted daughter of King Janaka
and our heroine.

SAGE VISWAMITHRA
(*VEESH-vah-MEE-tra*)
A sage with great supernatural
powers who trains Rama and
Lakshmana to become warriors.

RAAVANA
(*RAAAAAV-ana!*)
Lord of the Underworld and
our anti-hero.

MANDODARI
(*mun-DOE-dree*)
Raavana's loyal, virtuous,
eloquent, patient and generally
outstanding wife.

INDRAJIT
(*in-dra-JEET*)
Raavana's wise and learned son
who can become invisible in
battle.

VIBISHANA
(*vi-BEE-shna*)
Raavana's saintly brother.

SOORPANAKA
(*SURE-poon-akka*)
Raavana's tantrum sister who
discovers the power of love.

KING SUGREEVA
(*soo-GRIEVE-a*)
King of the monkeys who
makes a pact with Rama.

ANGADA
(*un-GAAD-a*)
A monkey who is Sugreeva's
nephew and potential heir to
the throne after his father, Bali.

HANUMAN
(*hun-oo-MUN*)
A monkey who is Sugreeva's aide.
Hanuman discovers considerable
powers when put to the test.

JAMBAVAN
(*JUM-bu-vun*)
King of the Bears who is famed
for his wisdom.

Other Characters

Book First

VISHNU
(*VEESH-noo*)
Lord of the Cosmos who
incarnates himself as Rama.

AGA
(*AAG-a*)
A forest-dwelling saint who
can turn viciously tiny when
he is disturbed.

TADAKA
(*TAA-da-ka*)
A female raksassy who enjoys
ruling over a . . . desert.

AHALYA
(*a-HULL-ya*)
The ideal woman created by
the gods.

GAUTAMA
(*GOW-ta-ma*)
Ahalya's mentor and then
her husband.

INDRA
(*EEE-ndra*)
A supreme god.

MANTARA
(MAAN-tara)
Queen Kaikey's loyal and
affectionate maid.

Book Second

QUEEN KAIKEY
(*kuy-KAY-ee*)
King Dasaratha's favourite wife
who is highly likeable till she's
made to feel vulnerable.

Book Third

VIRADHA
(*vi-RAAD-a*)
A gandharva (ogre) with an eye
for the ladies.

QUEEN KAUSALYA
(*cow-SUL-ya*)
Rama's mother who is loyal
to the king.

AGASTYA
(aGAAStya)
A great but now fallen sage
who is loyal to Rama.

BHARAT
(*BAA-rat*)
Queen Kaikey's wondrous son
who feels a great loyalty to Rama.

ILVALA
(*il-VAAL-a*)
A male raksassy with a taste
for sages.

SATROOGNA
(*sha-TRUE-gna*)
Twin brother of Lakshmana
with a matching shortness
of temper.

VITAPI
(*vi-TAAP-i*)
A male raksassy with a taste
for sages.

KING JANAKA
(*JUN-akka*)
Discovered Sita in a furrow
and claimed her as his daughter.

JATAYU
(*ja-TIE-you*)
Delightful Lord of the Vultures
who is loyal to Rama.

KORA
(*KOH-ra*)
Raavana's brother who is
horsey-faced and hot-headed.

MAREECHA
Son of Tadaka, and Raavana's
uncle. He is a shape-shifting
raksassy who is also a saint.

TRISHIRA
(*tra-SHEER-a*)
Kora's subordinate but no
less violent.

Book Fourth

TORAAPA
Buffalo king who seeks total
power. A lusty fellow.

TORAAPI
Son of Toraapa with whom
he fights. A lusty fellow.

BALI
(*BAAL-ee*)
Sugreeva's brother and one
of the mightiest creatures
to ever grace Earth.

TARA
(*TAAR-a*)
Bali's wife who then becomes
Sugreeva's wife. She is wise and
eloquent.

RUMA
(*as in 'rumour'*)
Sugreeva's wife who was
temporarily Bali's wife.

SAMPATHI
(*sam-PAAT-ee*)
A high-flying loveable vulture
and brother of Jatayu.

JAMBUMALI
(*jam-bu-MAAL-ee*)
Raavana's tusky ally.

PRAHASTA
(*pra-HUSH-ta*)
Raavana's commander-in-chief.

MAHODARA
(*ma-ho-DAA-ra*)
Raavana's lumpen ally.

VAJRADAMSHTRA
(*VAAJ-ra-DAAM-shtra*)
Raavana's blood-hungry ally.

DADDYMUCK
Tight-fisted owner of a vineyard.

VARUNA (*va-ROON-a*)
God of the Ocean who helps
Rama via Nala.

NALA (*NAAL-a*)
A gorgeously modest monkey
with a mighty power.

Book Fifth

PANURAT (*pa-NOOO-rut*)
A monster with border-patrol
skills.

VIDYUJJIVHA (*vid-you-JEEV-a*)
Raavana's glacial magician.

MATALI (*ma-TAAL-ee*)
A charioteer of the gods who
rides for Rama.

KOOMBARKANA (*KOOM-bar-
KAAN-a*)
Giant brother of Raavana with
a whopping appetite.

AGNI (*AAG-nee*)
God of Fire.

BRAHMA (*BRAA-ma*)
One of the holy trinity.

*Note: There is no global consensus on spellings of character names across
versions of Ramayana. Spellings vary according to local pronunciation;
I have selected spelling and pronunciation from several traditions.*

RAMAYANA

Prologue: Get Raaaaaaaaaavana!

The gods seek help from Vishnu after Raavana, having won great powers (boons), becomes destructive.

~

L ord of the Cosmos, Vishnu,
　　was brought back to heaven
from a stellar meditation
　　　　by many gods now stooped at his feet.

Said one, semi-stooped in the saffron light,
'O Lord, whilst we in thousand-day prayers
　　　　for peace are bent,
Raavana is bishboshing our kingdoms!'

Another god butted in, 'O Lord, with only a
　　　　　　　wink
he splash even our oceans into a coma.'

No wonder the gods were gurgling with collywobbles –

Raavana was toasting
> their earthly and galactic worlds!

By soaking the energy from everything he nulled
Raavana was now a supreme being becoming!

But who was this scallywag, this goonda?

Lord of the Cosmos, Vishnu, flashed
> umpteen visions to the gods
> that showed Raavana's path to glory.

In the first flashback, Vishnu displayed Raavana
> being born with ten heads
> and ten pairs of arms!

Then he showed Raavana, the teenager, on a hillock,

meditating

for so many non-stop years

> that smoke was issuing from his head

> and dulling the heavens!

The gods were constrained and had to grant Raavana
> great mental and physical powers

known as **boons**.

So many boons empowering Raavana

> that he could fly through the air

on the power of a thought alone.

Yet Raavana hankered after more boons,
so many boons that even Vishnu, according to natural law,
    had to hand them over.

Vishnu showed Raavana earning these boons by

fasting
atop a mountain

> dining only on the air's moisture

> for a hundred years.

> Boon-packed rock-hard Raavana was

> now shown standing on a toe

> without shifting a muscle

> through heatwave or

whirlwind! One

tough-nut

toe

whilst simultaneously

reciting Vishnu's beloved mantra

ommmmmmmmmmmmmmmmmmm

mmmmmmmmmmmmmmmmmmmmmmmm

mmmmmmmmmmmmmmmmmmmmmmmmmmm

for nine
hundred
solid years!

No surprise, in Vishnu's next vision, Raavana was losing

his mind

and was holding a blade
to cut off his own ten heads.

Vishnu, from on high, stopped him by asking
what he is wanting.
　　Raavana boomed back,
'Am I not a worthy King of the Universe, Lord?!'

Vishnu must have hoped Raavana would become
pure shanti, a bit like himself,

　　　yet soon as Vishnu's divine engine

　　　　touched

　　across each Raavana atom

in a somewhat unparalleled way

　　　Raavana went **bonkers!**

His ten heads, his ten sets of arm, trapezoid, rump, knuckle
　　　　and whatnot
　　　juddered tsunami-volcanically
　　　into a hardcore fierce firming-up!
　　　His every milli-inch was muscling –

　　　pinnacling with indestructibilitiness.

Roaring Raavana
simply leapt through
a spatial portal and
pegged it straight down
into the seventh, into
the lowest underworld,
Patala. The underworld
loaded with jewel-bubbling
        gardens
from where he brought up
the vile hoard of the race
known as

raksassy!

Vishnu's final vision displayed Raavana
        and his raksassy chums
lording it from an earthly island.

The gods pitched in chaos, chorused,
'What is to be done, Lord?'

Vishnu revealed a loophole in Raavana's boons.
        It's true Raavana sought immunity
        from demons and deities but he never
        sought immunity from mankind.

                So who's to say a man
                can't make him meet his maker . . .

Said a god, flabbergasted,
'How is it a measly ilk can dash him, Lord?'

Vishnu said that as the power bestower
he would become the power breaker.
He himself would end this havoc
    by incarnating himself
    as a human
    god-killing
    juggernaut.

Vishnu

v

Raavana

The gods gasped.
Said one, as much to himself,
'Lord, is it true you will turn into a meagre mortal . . . ?'

All gods dropped to their knees, lower much than before
      for Vishnu said that his conch
      and the wheel in his hands
      and the serpent coils he currently sat on
      would all be born on earth as his brothers!

And some of the gods here now . . . be born as monkeys.

A god checked his hearing and spluttered,
'Monkeys, my Lord? Is it monkeys?'

Vishnu explained that Raavana had been cursed
      in previous lives
to expect his end from man and monkey.

Said Vishnu, that as humans and monkeys,
      they would live normal-plus on earth –
      a tiptop team plotting
      against ever-toughening Raavana.

With his conch, wheel and coils, Vishnu
readied to find suitable couple
      seeking strapping male babies
      albeit with a tad complex background.

In the process, Vishnu hoped he may learn
what it feels being human.

Book First: Becoming Rama

~

Chapter One: I Need some Heir!

A king needs male heirs. A sage is sought to help the king's wives become pregnant.

~

King Dasaratha's broad open-mouth laugh
reflected a kingdom where it was the bog-standard norm
for all and sundry to enjoy their ample corns and golds

and have time on their hands for travelling
across the double-wide roads
on polished horses and elephants that wore frilly tattoos

    for no end of
festivals and general arty-crafty jocundity.

King Dasaratha's palace was in Kosala's capital, Ayodhya.
Ayodhya, famed for its tasteful stately mansions
    that were gaudy in gorgeous ways
    with jewels embedded to complement marble,
even modest homes were neat constructed so no leaks
    loosened the masonry.

And forgetting now the houses
would you please notice all about abounding
  nectars from sugarcane
  or palmyra for wicker-workery
  whilst the river Sarayu flowed
  mellow from the mountains
to lay at each Ayodhyan foot

  gems, flowers, sandalwood and peacock feathers.

Rose upward no war-fires
but many coloured smokes from fragrant incense woods, from
sacrifices and kitchen kilns for breads,
while steams performed their aerial sauna
when vegetables and meats tonked alike in the pot:

ecstatic bumper veggie and meat side by side harmony.
Nature loves mankind and puts itself on the plate!

  But why today, why was the king
  with his toddy tipple –
  why was he from pearly-teeth drollery
  utterly departed?

'My Lord, is it possible, your solar dynasty,
notwithstanding your three wives, is destined with no son
    to end?'
said a priest who'd been summoned by the king.

The mighty king, in despair, adding,
'My line – any-decent-how can it be saved?'

The priest recalled to himself an inner vision
which revealed help might be on its way
from one of the . . .
                    lords of the cosmos!

The priest advised, 'King Dasaratha, you must be ordering
a sacrifice
        to win the gods for your cause
        then your three wives
most likely can balloon with masculine babydom.'

The only sage with boost enough to flame a fertility sacrifice
        and best butter-up the gods
was bottom'd in the bowels of a mountain retreat.
                Meditating.

'Dear Priest, how best can I recruit this sage?
I know sages must no way be disturbed
        or their wrath may end one's life!
Especially if they are disturbed from their meditation.'

'Dear King, I have a plan to best recruit this sage.
        If reports about this sage are correct
        you must get hand-picking
the most beautiful damsels in your kingdom.'

The damsels were picked enough-quick

for Ayodhya abounds with super-beauteous damsels.
Said the priest,
    'Now send these super-beauteous maids
    for stirring out the hidden sage.'

The super-beauteous damsels
                traversed the valleys
           and the mountains,
      the woods and forests
to uproot the hidden sage.

The sage, who the damsels soon found and roused,
had never before seen a human, except his dad,
with only boars or goats for companionship.
So was he dazzled
        by the sweaty
           robe-flowing
               damsels!?

              He was almost cross-eyed
as he wondered what are these creatures . . . ?
Sensing straight off their double curves
and extra-ample legs and feathery but cut-back handsome
    eye-brows.
    How juicy his loins jostled!

He enjoyed wondering why their faces seemed painted:
were they born with vermilion lips and hunter-green
                lash lines?

His instinct was to put upon their gorgeous lips
    what juiced about his loins.
Tact his conduct kept up.
               Thankfully.

Despite the damsels distracting his meditation
the sage was far from upset and did not instant kill them.
Instead he see-sawed in a swoony mood
whilst being swept along by the jasmine-scented damsels

in a palanquin

    across the misty mountains

       then placed in Kosala,
in its capital, Ayodhya, and finally, in the king's hall.

The sage admired the king,
    a king whose creatures
    had such beauteous bodywork!
He felt flush-feeling for one maid greatly
         but would he be her magnet?
Luckily, the maid was drawn.

The sage bowed in admiration while the king said,
'She is your wife, on one condition:
that you for a year will brave a sacrifice
    with all its multiple tricky prayers
        to help me with my . . . issue.'

The sage couldn't begin his term soon enough!
One year braving
multiple tricky intensive mantras
        at the banks of river Sarayu.

At the end of which he grew a sacrificial fire
with clarified butter and spellbinding mantras.

    Kapow!

Shot up through the flames
        a vast chubby being in a white shirt
        with a hairstyle like the mane of a lion
and a golden medallion at his hairy chest.

This floating spirit held aloft a plate with special rice
which he placed before the king
        before swizzling
        head-first back down
        the fire.

Before departing with his beauteous bride,
the sage told the king, 'This rice is gharam-gharam.
A portion each, please, must be eaten now
        by your three wives!'

Lo and behold, skipping past a few moons,
look how the first wife is ballooning baby Rama,
the second, the king's favourite, ballooning Bharat,
and the third popping up with Lakshmana and Satroogna.

One morning, everyone awakes to hear
heavenly instruments twanging droll sounds across the sky.
And why so? It is the day of the same-day births
and no one knows the king's sons are:

> Lord of the Cosmos, Vishnu,
> the lord's serpent-seat
> the lord's divine wheel
> and his conch.

No one knows because the detail is not relevant. Only godliness
turned manliness is relevant.

Also relevant only is that the kingdom
is simply visiting and cooing:

> *what gorgeous boys!*
> *what gifted king!*

Chapter Two: Marriage/Mission

*Sage Viswamithra attends the king's ceremonial party and is
offered a gift of his own choosing.*

~

A stonking new hall built to honour the king
   and advertise his fit-for-marriage quartet boys
who have passed with flying colours
courses in spirit knowledge, law and latest science,
plus too sword fighting, archery and suchlike.

Into the hall for the ceremonial party
from the neighbouring states
comes each big wig, fat cat and hot shot
hoping his guava-yummy daughter
      be blessed
by the promise of a bold Dasaratha boy!

To pamper the king's prospects –
last guest in is a broad-foreheaded chunk-armed
      one-time warrior king
famed for his tough-guy leadership skills and ever-expanding

kingdom. He had renounced it all, becoming instead an air-
sucking sage.

On his arrival, King Dasaratha rushes forward,
the guests part away to hear the exchange,

'Sage Viswamithra.
What a fortune greeting the supreme sage.
My boys will be thrice blessed.
But please, from our salvers, come feast with us!'

'No need,' retorts the sage.
He has mastered bodies cravings, bodies stacked
famished pleadings for pamper and knick-knackery.
He is clean self-denial.
Uncomplicated male!

As the king's fate becomes assured by this guest's visit
custom demands a public gift; silence still,
'O Sage, it is an honour to be honouring you.
Please request whatever is befitting.'

The sage, knowing an honour will come on cue, says,
'I wish to perform a sacrifice
before the next moon.'

The sage knows how to steady
the storm to be stirred
by his party-pooper request
so he stirs it slowly,

'Sidhasrama, you know the place . . . beyond the Ganges.'

'But of course, it is the foul goondastan ground
bordering our kingdom. It has been dead-like since my sons
were born. Dead-like by those god-and-human hating
            arsoora.'

The king hooked. The sage stirs further,
            'Man-and-nature killing province.' The king

latches on, 'It smirches our kingdom.'

        'The gods are granting me powers
        to execute a gargantuan sacrifice.'

'Sage Viswamithra, how buoyed we all are
that you will float a classic sacrifice
at the site
where the resonant priests once plied their craft.'

        Applause from the audience.
        The sage stays quiet.

In steps

                the king, 'But what
the purpose of this sacrifice?
Would you jeopardise your life
before the teeth of raksassy and overhead arsoora?'

Now booming his voice somewhat (this one-time king):
'I seek to diminish these god-and-human eating
    arsoora and raksassy
    who not ever repent!

Our region once more will be safe for mankind.'

Again applause.

Words that act like arrows: unpullbackable,
once out in the unpluckable open, come from the king,
'But Sage, my army and I will ensure your safety,
I, myself, the army will lead and protect your praying.'

    The sage,
'You are too kind to support my sacrifice.
But only is needed one . . . sole person.
    Your son
    Rama
    is all,
    all
    -or-
    none.'

    'Rama?
    Rama
    mine
    stripling
    son!?'

The air in the room
kills itself into a brittle ice mirror
which is magnifying the king's tension wrinkles.
Yet how can he swallow his promise?
Or crack his pride before so many?

The king knows this goodly sage
is prodigiously versed in weapons unknown to all
except the gods
and may wish to hand these on to Rama,
yet he makes a final bid to keep
his connubially ripe, turned fifteen, son
by counting aloud the countless pleas
made to the gods for male heir . . . And now his heir
        slipping from sight!

The sage replies, 'Under my wings
      Rama will bear a princely stature.'

The issue boils down to kingly face-saving,
and honour, which gives a name its lustre,
'Rama has never been parted from his closest brother.
Lakshmana must go too.'

The sage agrees, then appeasing the king,
'Being at home, being in touching distance
      shows closeness in love
but if a seed is not removed, if it is made to sprout
at the heel of its parent tree
will it not be
stunted?

Will not Rama leave me also
　　　for what is becoming his correct trajectory?'

King Dasaratha's eyes glaze over.

He is remembering the day, aeons ago it was,
when he was out hunting.
As huntsman he was used to firing an arrow by hearing alone:
　　　sight not needed when you are a hotshot!

Except on this day,
whilst he was hidden in leaves and waiting for prey at a lake,
on hearing a splash

　　　　　　　　Dasaratha shot an arrow

into what he sensed was a deer.

Instead he heard a cry . . .

A boy's cry. A boy who had been carrying
two baskets on a pole
　　　　　each of which held his blind parents.

The frail blind dad touching his son's head;
through feeble tears, cursing the king,

　　　'I pray you learn too
　　　what it means to lose a son.'

In the stonking new hall, before his audience,
was all the king's great wit and wisdom mustered,
'Call my sons.'

Chapter Three: Kill that Mother!

*The boys enter a desert where they meet a raksassy. They are
then trained by the sage to become warriors.*

~

Perfect drought everywhere horizon'd in a desert.
   Heat licking heat
in a death-lust where only is growing Death.

Deep in the desert and somehow unfazed,
as if this were not miracle enough,
a mere boy wearing a divine blue demeanour
was steadfast walking. Nippy walker
whose feet were barely touching the ground
for the speed of his crossing too was unnaturally composed!

So who was this warrior-looking walker?
Rama, of course! Rama! The mighty boy
already with lithe but supernaturally powered limbs.

      Rama was being followed
      by his brother Lakshmana

and a bit behind was Sage Viswamithra.

They were north of Ayodhya
in the sun's anvil. A sun that slumped its deadening weight
on stone and rock
turning rock and stone into fine-spun sand.

     Gaps in the soil gaping.

The sun's anvil immobile
blurring the line

     between dawn   noon   evening.

     The bleach-bones strewn
     were from decayed animals.
Enormous horror jaws   gaped
into a frozen lunge after, even just one,

          wa
          ter-
          dr
          op. Into these dead jaws
had rushed
     the serpent and elephant alike for shade
     and died there. Fossilised tableaux.

The sage explained this was the sole way
to the sacrificial grounds, adding,

'Here was once a jolly peopled zone

with gardens and grounds, like bazaars, bright with fruits
  BUT
a demon family, a family of raksassy lived here once.
The couple had two boys who were born

  hippopotamusly tough!

As toddlers, the boy's larrikins involved
killing for the thrill! The big-head parents
  boasted of the edible end-product
the children's play-dates were becoming.'

The sage told the boys about a little saint, Aga,
who had his hut-home in the forest,
who felt compelled to cease the murder spree.
  He turned
  gnat-sized
  then flew
  at the neck

of this laughing-his-head-off braggart dad.
He flew at that mid-laugh neck
   whilst it was stretched
for it was easier to prod and puncture in a sec.

At his final breath the dad
  zipped about
like a wailing balloon when its air pours out
  then slopped alongside
  some redolent berries.

When Tadaka, the mum, and the brats spotted
their splatted fellow
they'd have swatted, in kind, this gimp saint,
but this gimp – where's he?

The gnat-sized saint
          buzzed a curse
that tore mum and the youngest brat from their former
physiques
into smudged
     malformed forms of themselves.
     Heart-stopping to stare at!

Saint Aga had deformed them into extreme versions
of their ogre states.

The young son scrammed and in scramming discovered
he had a wheeze
and had ankles shagged with spikes
so the boy not so much scrammed, as trudged
to loaf with arsooras in the underworld.

His dear brother, Mareecha, had got away
owing to the shape-shifting properties of certain raksassy.
Mareecha was beautiful at switching into a deer,
and had sneaked away for Raavana's kingdom.

Said the sage, 'I have a dread fear
Mareecha will cross your path again, one day.'

Rama was unperturbed
as the sage shared news about the mum
who was cursed to live alone,
'. . . in this forest which she turned to a desert
        by her single gift:
        the gift of breathing ill fires.
        She's called a scorcher . . .

If her sons were strong as ten hippos each
Tadaka is rampant as a hundred hippos.
And her diet being raw humans
        she's called a man-eater.'

The boys smiled nervously as the sage sniffed the air.
'Tadaka pierces anything alive with her spiky trident.
Not even here will you hear the shrill beetle
or any tweeting sweetie bird. All been spiked.
Tadaka roams here still. My vow of
non-violence means you must step up.'

The sage stood Lakshmana back with him
for it was clear Rama was being tested.
Rama pleaded,

        'Where is she?'

Before the sage answered the question,
the question was being answered

by a rackety storm
ploughing towards the sage and the boys.

What formed through the ploughing, before Rama,
was a normal-size woman
        but with eyes gobbing fire,
                with fangs dribbling molten.
All of it hung on an old mama
bereft of her boys and her husband.

Good grief!

Rama felt her blue-mood
when he used the word 'mother' on asking the sage,
'This poor mother – how should I kill her?'

Said the sage, 'You must not be considering her
as woman. Think not she is woman. Think only the epitome
she presents you.'

The thought struck home.
Though Rama ached for his three mums'
hugs
he knew 'mum' was not the warrior word
and hardened as recipient
of this fiend's three-pronged spear

which came at shrill speed
                for his brows
and arrived within eye-shot

just in time for Rama's nimble-fingered
    stringing of his massive bow
so his arrow flew just in time
      to shatter

h e r   s   P   e
                a

                   r!

The shattered spiky shards flew up
        and gaining speed
        rained sharply down
        into the mum
        stabbing her
        in her tender
        flesh-parts.

Tadaka was dead.
    Hoisted with her own petard.

Spectating overhead
the gaggle of ebullient gods
made life move fast-forward across a once desolate region.

They made flowers plurp into dandy lives of purples and tangs
shaded by newly sprung panasa, palm and mango trees.

The gods chimed into the sage's inner voice,
'Grant this fine-handed boy the deepest know-how.
    He may be the saviour!'

Over the coming seasons, upon his willing wunderkind
the sage delivered the subtlest A to Z techniques
so both Rama and Lakshmana mastered
the art of defence, and if necessary, attack.

Rama perfected the hardest mantras,
that once recited
allow you to ignore those gobby rogues:
      Hunger, and her dry beau, Thirst.

Rama was fast becoming awesome:
he could shoot an arrow exact through ninety palm trees
        to pierce a juicy apple
and could shift a hill
      or heave-ho an irksome cliff.
But he had to master restraint
      for the sage advised against causing a stink
on nature's blossom harmony.

Said the sage, as he sat midst crags,
'I will now teach you bala and antibala mantras.
These are essential for martial know-how. Once mastered
you will gain instant insight to select the good path
from the gnarled entangled junctures.
Plus too, when asleep you will be shielded from demons.'

The sage next taught them how to hone mental focus
for summoning and harnessing the Dev Astras,
that is to say, the snazziest weapons of the gods
that can only be activated by mantras. Mantras only

can return the weapons or else utter chaos
when weapons back-fire!

And mastery of a mantra leads to best tool control.
What a bruising time
      that left the boys with singed limbs and digits
when they practised conjuring Astra weapons
because some could be hot as hot coals
               and some mere
               smoke-wisp.

When the boys were really skilled
it became a cinch, a doddle, sending back each Astra
         to its celestial shelf!
The sage then loaded Rama with weapons
for the journey. Trooping through the air

out of nothing

were brand-new weapons of shiniest divine-gold
paraded before Rama, as if to say,
'Lord, we are yours to command.'

Not forgetting Lakshmana who also earned
with flying colours blades, spear-like missiles
     and diamond-set scabbards
to rival Rama's that stood at his feet, as if to say,
'Lord, we are yours to command.'

Chapter Four: Our Exchequer Ganga

Sage Viswamithra relates the importance of nature.

~

'Just as our stories recall and revive our long line,
   so it is we only attain greater knowledge of our circumstances
once we feel the earth we are
daily sharing.

My dear boys, every inch of the earth
      is a divine memory.
As one of the five original elements
Mother Earth has been here from the off.

Though each human trace is erased
      from the universe and the Earth,
though each corpse be million years under,
Mother Earth will always bear
an impress of every foot that trod anxiously
and ecstatically, through good and evil, upon her . . .
Upon her . . . till Kala consume all again.

And what of Ganga? Ganga is the greatest necklace –
    its riches draping our world.
Just look at her streams flowing down from the Himalayas
and kissing all they touch
for blooming essence of rare herbs and wild fruits.
Ganga feeding all that beards and garbs the earth.
    Ganga nursing the parched throat
        dying for a sip.

The souls of each being are cleansed for salvation
once their ashes replenish the roots
    by flowing through water.
    Ganga rushing down cleansing
and bearing so each stitch touched
        becomes, in essence, holy!

'Herein is life is death is life and death and life again.'

The wizened sage was speaking from within
the mist-covered wood on a mountain height
and as the mountain exhaled its tender vapours
the sky was calmed
    and calmed too were the boys
    who were soothed into sleep.

Chapter Five: Utter Foul Sacrifice

Sage Viswamithra attempts to make his sacrifice.

~

Now from the highest mountain peak
in Sidhasrama, said the sage,
'We have been travelling across the great heights
for only a dozen sunsets, or so it seems,
but many seasons have elapsed
and how well you have fought for insight
in yoga, philosophy and the ways of demon destruction.

Here is where we will perform the great sacrifice.
We must toil to attain our vision's purpose.'

The sage went high-low preparing,
and the brothers brought cartloads of sages
        from near and far
who themselves had been busy propitiating the gods
for this culminating battle.

The rabble of arsoora and raksassy

43

was running about in the sky
like feet tapping on the floorboards upstairs.
Their pongy rain indicated to the brothers
an attack on the sacrifice was getting dirty.

The sages lit fire from a hundred-plus trees
and circled it with chorus prayers
so song and flame ascended with a pomegranate brightness.
But what came down from above
were distress cries from supposedly tortured children.
Each trauma or sorrow was reconstructed by the demons
and played aloud. Endless mimic voices.
Horror radio! Psycho crèche . . .

The demons, who lived in the lowest regions
of the ooper-world, were scuppering the sacrifice.
The sages felt unduly boo-hooey
at the next set of mimic-whines

    from sisters, mothers, grandmothers
supposedly under attack:

whose shadow is at my nape

    release my wrists fiiiieeeendd

    my sons will   *my husband is coming*

HARAAMZADAAAAH!!!

The demons were having a wild time.
To further unsettle the prayers
they thrashed down vat-load

STOMACHS

spleens

giblets

blood-water

GORE GALORE!

A gonad fell in a sage's outstretched palm,
urine dribbled the beard of another . . .
The delicacy of the story forbids further embellishments
of this nature, save to say
many an abattoir must have been ransacked and spilled
        at devious intervals.

    The battle was hotting up
    so Rama made a solid promise,
'Belt out your prayers about this spiring fire . . .
    We will shelter you.'

Rama and Lakshmana fled
        to different mountain ranges
and became pure arrow action
        shooting thousands of spears at dizzying speed,

so many arrows

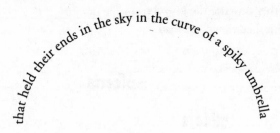

that held their ends in the sky in the curve of a spiky umbrella

shielding the sacrificial fire
        from being doused or spattered.

So long as each multiple-arrow-round made a penumbra
    the sacrifice stayed prayer-happy.

The desperate demons resorted to earth eruptions
    that flung lava.
Lava, mimic-cries, gassy stinks and suchlike malarkey
    were thinning, were fading . . .

Somehow the sages were pulling off the sacrifice
with extreme-focus imbrication of mind and body
till each sage was a flame-ball burning evil from earth!

May this story be forgiven for digressing
but dear Sages
please do not be forest-firing too much
this cuddly planet whilst engaged in an anti-demon combat:
    who would rather not be harbouring a floorboard of evil
    than be losing their home sweet home?

Returning to our story,
now that the region was freed from the demons,

in the place of eruptions were wide-ranging rainbows
        because peace was advertising itself
as promoted by the mountain-to-mountain-wide calling-card
        of spangly colours.

Rama, Lakshmana and the sages saw, flying
through the rainbows,
and couldn't help but wave
                        at, the birds, birds, birds.
Even cheeky cuckoos.

Chapter Six: Rocky Woman Show Up!

Rama revives the ideal woman and contemplates her story.

~

On the outskirts of Mithila,
a fabled city where they would rest and meet its king,
the sage took the boys past a neglected ashram.

Rama, by the entrance, walked over a raised
slab-stone. No sooner had he touched the stone
than the stone was enlivened by his foot.

Before him the stone whirled upwards
into the image of an immaculate curvaceous woman.
The curvaceous woman
appeared a mirage at first
then fleshed into a miracle
of flesh and blood!

She stooped before Rama, and poured from her
　　　ocean wafts and tender flower scents,

　　'May the Lord bless your feet.
　　That you are rooted at heart.
How long I have felt this broad-sided justice. '

　　Not looking
in the slightest way stirred, Rama turned
to Sage Viswamithra and enquired after the woman.

Said the sage, 'This ideal beauty is Ahalya.
　　Formed by the gods
then raised here on earth by her mentor, Sage Gautama.'

The sage told Rama, it was natural
that Gautama and Ahalya wed
　　when they fell head-over-heels.
Once married they were the perfect brain-to-brawn couple
　　ever-after.

But one of the supreme gods, Indra it was,
been always horny for Ahalya. He lost self-control.

One day, as Gautama went for his river wash
and prayers at the bank
　　Indra was like a cloud ready to burst!
And burst he did by spilling down to earth
as Ahalya's husband. Exact-same copy.

But hornier! Horny as
Ahalya and Gautama on their marital night.

Ahalya was naturally enough most pleased
and surrendered screaming her great jollification.
As the first round of the intercourse peaked

through the woods

Gautama cottoned on to

Ahalya's
fabric-tearing
lust-cries.

He was hot on the cry trail and arrived home
watching a bed couple bonking
for round two! An eyeful for an eye fool!

Gautama saw the buttocks of some poltroony fellow
leap off his missus and turn into a cat
sneaking off for a cat-flap. Gautama said,
'O cat, I say it – cursed be your body,
covered all over with rude-appearing slits!'

The cat meowed away, freckled with rude-appearing slits.
Indra would become the butt of jokes in heaven.
He would brood in a lock-up with darkness for a friend,
neglecting his worlds. Brahma would eventually forgive
repentant Indra by blinking each of those slits into a gem.

Most gods are not so lucky winning forgiveness
no wonder Indra's called the Gemmy God!

Back to Gautama, who was still bristling – now with his wife,
'Lateral lecher, I say it! I have not satisfied you too much?
May your frisky features turn into a
                                    lateral
                              granite
                    floor-slab!'

Ahalya's pleadings were off the pace:
she was humiliating herself by saying,
'Who's the real Gautama?
How is it, that cat was my husband?'

                    Too damn late it all was . . .

Ahalya felt a silicon feeling sludging slowly
        through her feet and upwards
her joints senseless firming slabby.

Gautama sensed he may have been stung
by a charso-bee, poked by a hornswoggle: in short, duped!
He pitied his pleading wife
and sneaked-in a get-out clause,

'Ahalya, I say it – your salvation
        may it one day come at the feet of Rama.'

The sage then waited for Rama to speak.

Rama, stock-still,
by the ashram which was overgrown with shadows, said,

'What is it in nature's diurnal housing,
nature's inward store and safe-keeping
that it take to its heart something
     wished into nothing?

Why or how does this, the mightiest of all, Nature,
revive desolate

     ash

into scented being again?

What is this pulsing beneath my feet
     that knows what I do not?

What am I become
     if I would not bless
what nature would not immaterialise?'

The sage pressed for more,
'But nothing is in itself, Rama . . .'

'It appears this woman was taken
from the sacred vows of marriage
by another man, albeit a god in mortal form.

     Could Gautama keep her at home

and permit his reputation's casting out?

Yet Ahalya has served her punishment.

> I say, let us be measured
> only by the path we intend.'

Gautama, had been amidst thorns, behind the ashram,
praying for Rama these years.

> He now rose
from his hunched state and was watched
lighting up like a starry night. He was seeing his wife –
his wife with a lavanyakam flower in her hair

nearing . . .

The perfect pair hugged to the pealing bells in the distance.
Rama blessed them so their minds
> be meted for fresh beginnings.

If only all our world's misunderstandings
were blessed by Rama
and our failed loves could begin, with stars in their eyes, again.

Book Second: The Marriage Bow

~

Chapter One: Was that Love at First Sight?

Rama arrives in Mithila and is struck by a woman on her balcony.

~

Fan your imagination on Ayodhya's look-alike: Mithila
   with its towers   turrets   domes
                all golden or pastel,
and in a gentle season
                the ground glittering with cast-off
jewellery –
   a snapped necklace dashed mid-dance,
or nuisance diamonds during a passionate embrace

   discarded!

And no Mithilan craving to bag the casual
                chucked-away pearl
for such is the manner of the rich among the rich
in caring sharing Mithilan fertility,
       that perfect match for an Ayodhyan.

Rama and Lakshmana fanning their gaze
on swings strapped to trees swaying with couples
and nearby, the girls
    wore a length of keshauma cotton
        that whirled about the body
            and pointed
            to the S type
                    anklets.

And pointed to the bell-topped toe-ring on each toe,
each toe-ring specially designed to suit that toes' darling mien

and speaking a while longer of toe-rings
some girls wore the cheeky come-on rings that were
        double-bosom'd
            and filled with a
            tinsy knocker
dingling its own tantalising tune, *hiehie!*

What's more, all girls strode about wondrously barefooted!
All rehearsed love tunes or danced to soft gomgoms,
no wonder Rama and Lakshmana
smiled to the music of their hooting, their panting!

The brothers walked past the hotshot array
            of wide-moustached
culgee-turbaned archers come from near and far
to put their pinging bows to the test. And there,
whilst by the stream, Rama's

eyes lifted upwards

and there across on a balcony
from where the cool breeze blew off the balmy sea

a woman in shining
kausheyam silk
with a spotted deer border
and with eyes brilliant as the lotus
and with her feet all of a sudden rooted
so she looked the double of the goddess Lakshmi!

Rama's second take
on who is that, is that
the beauty of the world
across on the balcony
observing the jamboree . . . ?
And her eyes fell
according to the exact second of the cosmic dial
that we call fate,
on Rama's eyes
at the same time
as Rama's had flown
startled upon hers.

Their heartbeats doubled on the same count
and harkened in a shared breath.

The harkening damsel was

Sita

who was taking in her familiar Mithilan view
when she fell on a feeling of greater familiarity
punctuated by the sorrow of utter unknowing.

Whilst Rama dazed at her beauty, Sita dazed at his

and thought to herself how this must be
the veiled recognition
        that we call love at first sight.

Together they had walked, aeon after aeon,
fresh as bold new lovers, under the starry lanes
        in heaven:
he as Vishnu and she as Lakshmi.

'Twas in this incarnation,
under all the depredations a human endures,
        and a lapsed memory
being amongst our most humbling torments,
through which each looked upon the other:

        a stranger.

When Rama disappeared from view, Sita felt
a withering
for her heart had absorbed a love dart!

Wounded by love, virgin love, she remained.
The bangles on her wrists slumped downward till,
by her attendants, she was spread on a soft bed
far from the formal mood sought by her obligations.
She was heard murmuring,

'. . . emerald shoulders . . . blue-sky beauty . . .

who are you?
           why have you invaded me
pinching my heart to leave me ashamed?

i wish you stood before me now as a god…

only to you   i feel i would freely   speak my mind . . .'

Her maids lit cool lamps,
whose wicks were soothed with clarified butter,
they found even this flame proved intolerable
and Sita survived only by soft light so the maids tempered
the darkness with spread-about luminous gems.

Dark rings fringed her eyes.
When she moaned that her bed was not soft
her maids made her bed on a plate of moonstone
with layered softest petals
           but the flowers wilted.

Ache prolonged agonised writhing ache.
Darkened days and nights left her quizzing,

'Was he only hallucination . . .'

And Rama? Enough to say,
when at the lodgings, he sensed his whole being
being sacrificed to a girl with curly locks across her forehead!
Rama wondered if she was married
but if she were
would he have felt such a fine dart of desire?

On one whose bow was schooled in the art
of demonology, on one whose bow depended
demon death,
now fondling his mind with a girl in flowing silks for armour,
with a bow of sugarcane and flowers for arrows,
how could she so softly have felled him?
Rama smiled at the irony.

Chapter Two: The Marriage Bow

*King Janaka seeks a husband for his daughter. Rama must
shoot an arrow to win himself a bride.*

~

Sage Viswamithra introduced the boys to King Janaka.
He knew the king of Kosala would be struck
by royal stock turned warriors armed with weapons.
Indeed, the king, straight off, considered Rama
             a fitting match
for his daughter.

One drawback, the king had a massive arrow-bow
and guess what, the king had set a condition
that anyone man enough to pluck his daughter
would first have to pluck up their manliness
        by one: lifting the rather large bow
        two: bending it
        three: stringing it
        and fourthly: shooting an arrow
so, fifthly and ultimately, becoming a stunner's lover ever-after!

The sage was hardly surprised to hear
countless suitors had failed the big five,
turned stroppy then stormed the palace
      to make off with Sita.

Charming.

The king mourned his ambitious condition,
'The elect man, or such a one, must win Sita.
You know, Sage, she was not from a human born.

I am reminded all this
      world belongs to Mother Earth.
      Only in the fancy of a mirrored mind
do these belongings become subject to a pomp kingdom.

Once upon a time
      I zigzagged through clumpy mango
          and guava groves
traipsing through banana plantations to reach a stone-field.
It was there I sought to bless the earth
      and our peoples with peace.
Using a rough old ditched plough
I cracked the barren with straight furrows.
Not stopping till the sun was behind the citrus trees
when from a furrow I heard a sound. Of crying.

Tired and panting, I delved the furrows
and soon found what my blade had brought out:
        a baby.

64

A radiant baby girl
borne by warm earth whilst cradled on a wooden arch.
    I lifted up the naked baby.
Suddenly the ground cracking, laboured aside

    as the arch lifted upwards!
The arch creaking out wider and wider till it rocked
        gently and fully upon the earth.

    A giant bow, it was, with a golden string.

Imagine a bow being nature's umbilicus.
From a deadly weapon sprung cuddly life.
I swaddled the baby that my wife and I had craved.
We named her after her birth place: Sita: furrow.'

The sage seemed unsurprised and suggested,
'Are there divine tinkerings in birth and bow matters?
Perhaps the gods favour you in some way.
Would you bring the bow out for Rama to inspect?'

Locked in a box and smouldering with aloeswood smoke,
the bow was hoicked on eight pairs of enormous wheels.
It was so huge it proved incomprehensible in one view:
unless you stood off you'd never see it whole!

The onlookers feared that the king rather keep his Sita at home
and free from some regal dunderhead –
why else be harsh with his conditions?
They worried for Rama that he must lift the bow.

A gong rang out for Rama to pluck the bow.
The audience watched him calmly measure it up.
They closed their eyes and hummed prayers
    to bother the imminent crush
    but to their great mystification
the boy was raising the weapon and placing it on a toe.

The bow, wide as a rainbow, was being drawn inward
under the non-stop force of Rama's grip on the golden string.
Gosh!

Rama kept at it till the arrow, heavy as a tree,

    got blasted into the clouds

and who couldn't hear, when the bow tips touched,

its concussion cccccrraaaccKKKK

as it shattered like two mountains rent apart.

And who couldn't see the firework display –
the flying bow-shards exploding through the eminence!

Having missed some man-to-be in his fullest to-do,
Sita still pined for her balcony scene. From where she watched
perfumes being sprinkled
and people donning their best and dancing at the palace gates
relieved the king's judgement had been judicious,

that a fit lad would meet his match. How cool!

Cool enough that the gods
hovered earthward, in human form,
and mingled among the humans who were
dancing the sandalwood-sprinkled night away!

Chapter Three: Choodamani

The wedding of Rama and Sita.

~

Is there anything gaudier, more glorious or heart-breaking
    than a good old-fashioned wedding?
The husband will henceforth be nourished by a wife
but the bridal parents must relinquish the breakfast hugs
a daughter has daily blessed upon them.

A wedding is sighs, a wedding is laughter,
a wedding is footloose arms-in-the-air clamorous *enjollament*,
a wedding is
            Rama's father receiving a jolly invite
from King Janaka
for a bride and groom embarking on their belle vie,
'so kindly come with all your peoples to celebrate'.

On the sandy streets of Ayodhya, on the streets of Mithila
who is not hearing the elephant-loud trumpeting,
            All you beauties please be coming
            by-and-by to partying party party!

Suddenly the whole of Ayodhya
on the streets ready for the trek to the kingdom of Kosala.
When the huge mass assembled
          then shuffled onward
it seemed as though the world was in procession
surging like the waves and tides of the Ganges.

The gathering can be summarised by admiring the youth:
     when a boy fell off his horse
and into a palanquin, and into the arms of a honey-smelling
lover –
the lover didn't sting him with a slap
instead they spun themselves into laugh aloud gupshup
and would not need parting,
               couples in a strop
               soon patched up,
and dumbbell-armed lads stood by a river
offering to carry across their dreamboat,
the dreamboat that sought no better transportation!

Camels were happy with their necklace sacks
of margosa leaves to moisten the parched throats
so they continued wearing that comedian smile.
All listened to proud talk about wondrous Rama
     winning the most beautiful woman
     as proved by the ultimate praise
          that this Sita
          had thighs
          shapely as
          elephant trunks.

Four days jollity later, they arrived at King Janaka's capital
　　　to the sounds of bugles and gomgoms.
The miles-long line of the party on the royal road
was embraced into homes, palaces and camps
as the heart-strings of Ayodhya strummed
　　　along with the heart-strings of harpy Mithila.

　　　　The two kings met
and in an instant two powerful states were bonded,
for marriage is not about two people
but about two tribes forging fellowship,
couples commingling their communities
　　　so affection's commerce
　　　　is forever being overlapped
and broadened in the great flow of humanity at one.

A father was escorted to meet his son
and that father, King Dasaratha, pumped with pride at Rama
whose stature now seemed manly.

Then, amidst the carousing, came the big day.
Rama, with his robes as though dipped in saffron,
blazing along on the Royal Elephant in fullest paraphernalia
　　　through the ecstatic streets.

On the marriage platform, Janaka offered flowers, incense
　　　and other symbols of health and wealth.
A sacred fire was kindled and incantations rang out.
Then Janaka brought in his daughter.

The congregation gasped because Sita
seemed the double of Lakshmi who had stood upon a lotus.
Sita's kausheya-silk dress was gold and the edging raised gold
which was woven close as inseparable swans.

Janaka held a round pearl on a gold leaf, the Choodamani,
then he placed it in Sita's hair above her forehead.
The Choodamani was a crown serving the elect face.

When Sita was alongside Rama, Janaka spoke,
'Here is my Sita. In giving Sita I give my ground.
Look at her. Never tire of looking at her.
Take her hand in your hand
and evermore she will walk alongside you
as your own shadow walks alongside you.'

On the marriage platform, Rama's heart-stopping moment:
he observed for the first time his bride.

He who had lifted a godly bow
became woozy with fear and wonder:
would this be the beauty of the world
that he had observed, that day on her balcony?

As he lifted the veil, to his great release,
he saw once again the face that had completed his being
    now complete his being once again
        as he hoped it would for ever more.

Impossible to imagine how she felt

as she wondered upwards to observe
the face, the exact-same face,
she had once seen from her balcony
                    beaming at her, again!

The face that had made her senseless
        now made her deepen with ocean-scented aromas
        as though she were flown atop a lotus leaf.

Chapter Four: Lady in Waiting

Mantara worries for Queen Kaikey's future.

~

Mantara, the whisperer and dream-pot stirrer
who maddened sleep. Mantara, the soothsayer
dire! Mantara, with her high back,
made forecasts that made news on the stands
that struck you between the eyes!
Mantara the maid, Queen Kaikey's trusted maid.

King Dasaratha's favourite wife, Queen Kaikey,
knew from Mantara that the wizened king had been
hearing
howling torments
    on the spines of comets.

Queen Kaikey knew from Mantara that astrologers
had predicted the king's stars, that Mars and Jupiter
        were aspecting the same house,
in other words, his numbers were nearly up.

The king had then suddenly announced he would spend
     his last days throne-free.

The queen knew Rama would be next on the throne,
and good job too. Rama was being readied for the throne,
     albeit in great haste.
'Twas then, Mantara rushed in to see Queen Kaikey.

Something was on Mantara's mind. She began mockingly:
'Why is Rama's mother giving everyone gold gifts?
     Has she come into another fortune?'
The queen merely grinned. The king's three wives were equals.

Next move, but a tad more direct, 'Why is it
you skip around
     like a girl? Have you reckoned fully your future?'
Despite Mantara's weird mood, the queen held out
a diamond necklace gift
     to celebrate Rama's great fortune.
Said Mantara, 'What, is this Rama your son?'

No response again. Then very direct, risking everything,
     Mantara smashed the jewels
     down at the tiles!

Sweet Queen Kaikey, in her regional accent, japed,
'You are getting picky-dicky, Mantara . . .
Is my taste too old-fashioned for you?'

'It is not jewels I need. My dear Queen,

76

like that necklace, you too will soon be on the ground . . .'
'That is a very hard fall for me, Mantara.'

Instead of heeding the queen, the queen's jugular
was felt to be up for grabs by a calmer voice now,

    'Your beauty
    my beloved Queen
    and your youth,
as I'm sure you know, are your glittering prowess.
But beauty, like a torrent, like youth,
rushing down the mountainside as it upends flowers and leaves
might for the duration
       hold the observer in a spell.
When it passes,
       or lies slumped like a heap of mess,
what is left? After youth and the passing of beauty?

Dear Queen, in its place you will be a sandy bed!
When the diamonds about your delicious neck
    highlight your wrinkles,
when your most kissable cheeks
sag like cheap ear-rings
      you will be counterfeit!

A bad copy, not stirring recognition of former glamour.
Plunder and oblivion. Plunder and oblivion
      brushing you aside
with the back of the king's hand or the king's children's
hands.

You will be, as other queens before you,
ring-fenced far away from your darlings and your darling
king.'

Queen Kaikey pushed Mantara for more,
       'Give me a mirror.
What? Have I slept so bad last night
that my face is chip-chopped by the choppiest sea-wrinkles?'

Mantara, who had raised the queen,
cut in,
       'Where is Bharat? Your own dear son?
Why was he recently dispatched to your father's house
when the future of Ayodhya is finding new feet?

       Why is he not making his stand?'

The queen leapt up, alarmed by her own lively activity:
'Wonderful news! Rama is becoming king
and are you not mortaring and pestling some fresh
       clove-scented mischief?'

'My sorrow is for the doom that overhangs you.
It reminds me of the little dove entering
                  the jaws of a wildcat.
Dear Queen, I was there once,
back in the days when the middle-aged king sought you,
late one night he was at it persuading your father
that despite his
age this teenage girl should be his bride.

And how did he persuade your father?
Well I overheard our king promise him
that your firstborn would overleap his other sons
and become king – in return for your hand!

And that is how you were won.'

Queen Kaikey sensed her skin ripple with wrinkles,
or fear of them at least. Her frail retort,

'I do not see the difference between Rama and Bharat.'

'So why is it your dancing feet seem so heavy?
Rama will banish your own Bharat or break him
    or behead him!
You will be untouchable in your status
    of an ex-
    queen
    of an ex-
    king.

At best, you will be stooped to a heel
serving Rama's giddy, gold-gift-wafting mummy-jee
who would love to be chucking, like yesterday's rice,
    the kings favourite dish.'

'Never. How dare she even rise to it!'
Thus the queen was contracted.

Chapter Five: Two Wish

Queen Kaikey tells the king she would like to claim her wishes.

~

King Dasaratha hurried to fill in Queen Kaikey
that soon as tomorrow Rama would be king
and could he, the ex-king, book a date
    for gadding about
    the cucumber garden with his no.1 queen?

    His silken joy felt burred
when he heard the queen was holed in the Bile Room,
an annexe part of the palace where you could cool off:
a posh shed kept purple, unkempt, with serpent skins.

He walked into the Bile Room and saw Queen Kaikey
with kohl smudged, like ash, on her upper cheeks,
    wild roaring hair as though tugged
by chimps. Yet to the king she was still his
        Naga goddess!

In the gloom, the king apologised

for not telling her the great news sooner.
He wondered what anger she was burning off.

'Dust and rags have become my fate.'
Her luscious voice roused the king into youthly moods.
'But Queen, let us drive about in our chariot
          waving at the revellers.'

Futile hope. He sat on a footstool by the queen
and heard her insist he give her her due.
'You remember the battlefield,
in that war between the gods, when you rose to the high
heavens
to rescue the mighty-fighty Indra
and found yourself prickled with arrows?

It was I who drove you from the dark fields
          and plucked arrows out from you.'

Suddenly his sizzling joints ached:
he couldn't look at the queen
          for her beauty was making him idle:
she seemed a goddess lowered from the heavens
          and hunkered in the Bile Room.

'Yes, my Queen, I remember it well.
Any chariot would have killed its wheels over me.'
'I nursed you, keeping you safe from public gupshup.'
The king solemnly replied,
'I have not forgotten nor will I ever.'

'You remember you insisted on two wishes.
You said I must have what is pleasing my heart.'
'I did, indeed.'

Always when he came back tired from court
Queen Kaikey never sought details or meddled
but waited at the doors to tickle him with tender hugs . . .
And mostly for this she was his
favourite wife. How unlike herself she was now, so stiff,

'I was not intending ever to request my wishes.
But I shall ask for my wishes now.
If you refuse, you will be the first of the descendants
of the Sun God to go back on your word.
Monarchs, all, will shun you. Common people will laugh at
you.

You have heard it tell of Saibya –
to keep his promise to a hawk he cut the flesh
clean away from his own bones and flung it to that bird.'

'Fear not, Queen. Speak freely.'
The queen took a deep breath and found herself
        speaking her wishes,

'Crown our son

        Bharat

            king.

Banish
Rama.

Banish Rama deep in the forest for fourteen years.'

    Staggering to
    his feet
the king looked faint.
He seemed blinded in the way he looked away,
'Will the kings not shun me as a foolish dotard?
Rama will do as told for he never acts in two ways . . .'

The queen was now unstoppered,
'Send presently a messenger to bring home Bharat.
And tell Rama to begin his fourteen years.'

With his eyes still shut, the king whispered,
'Are you a demon?' 'Don't you curse me, King!
I never asked you to come looking for me with your glee.
Go back to Rama's mother.'

And so they spent the night to-ing and fro-ing
in insults and attempts at persuasion by the king.
The night ended in the Bile Room;
a queen on the floor, a glorious king on a broken couch.

Chapter Six: God Bless the . . . King . . . ?

Rama is informed of the king's wishes.

~

The roaring coronation fire put out,
   the crowded guests
for Rama's anointment were informed the ceremony
would be delayed and, worst of all,
Rama's date with kingly fate was now kaput!

Rama's favourite elephant, Shatrunjaya,
dropped his head in despair and beat his feet.
Gossip blushed each man's cheek
that the sweetest of queens, Queen Kaikey, was to blame.
Rama met the king and Queen Kaikey,
the king meekly cried out, 'Rama.' then left.
The king was bad out of shape, he was like a deer
trembling before a rumbling-belly tigress.

Queen Kaikey took charge of the two wishes,
'It is your duty to help your father keep his word.
You must stay away for the full fourteen term,

returning along with Sita, if you take her, only then.
The king prays your sojourn is safe. Is uneventful.'

Rama listened as Kaikey continued,
'All the while you must be adorned
in tree-bark and deerskin only.
And live on the fruits and roots you've plucked.

If you do not satisfaction these terms
you will shame your father

in this and further worlds.

It is your duty as a son.'

Rama broke down the shock,
piece by piece, within himself

and absorbed all

without a single question, replying,

'I do not crave office. I am happy finding kinship
in the forest. My only sorrow is that, since a father
is divinity incarnate to his children,
could not my father, my guru, break me
this news?'

Rama wasn't expecting an answer. Nor got one.
The queen, so distraught at having to execute the strong arm,

longed for a long spell in the Bile Room. Especially
when Rama added, 'I want to assure you
I am not pained at all by your decision
which is for the best, I believe.
Only promise me you will keep my father
from sorrow at our parting.'

Rama had never see the queen so unknown to herself,
    'You must leave at once.'

Over the coming days, after Rama had left, the king
was troubled. Became inert. Except when he heard a footstep,
he would ask, 'Has Rama come?'

No mollycoddling from Rama's mother, Kausalya,
could rekindle the king. The thought of Rama and Sita,
    and Lakshmana out there somewhere
on the violent forest rough beyond the bamboo clusters
    dressed in tree-bark
was crushing for King Dasaratha.

                He weakly craned his
neck, straining his eyes to fill them with returning Rama,
dreaming the fourteen years might have elapsed.

As reported by the master poets of Rama's yarn
and interpreted in the world's tongues
        time and time again,

the God of Death, Yama,
reached into King Dasaratha's breast
and felt it time to summon out his mortal soul
as diamond bells fell sweeping a soft song across heaven.

Chapter Seven: Fate

Rama and Lakshmana dispute over what they should do next.

~

Hotshot ninja warrior, evil's nemesis,
 sidekick to the chief demon slayer
and ideal brother: Lakshmana was ready
to bladder-bust his gutless crown-pilfering brother, Bharat!

Lakshmana was behaving like a solo orchestra:
he was percussioning his armour-clad arms
and twanging his bow-strings like crashing comet sounds,
then for finale he threw umpteen trees in such an uppity
        they clacked ice in the distant rocks.

Eventually in the garden where the peacocks had been preened
and flower displays tiered,
with the fountains set at highest possible jet
                        for the coronation
was where Rama found Lakshmana.

Said Rama, 'It seems you are wanting to show the world

what a wildcat warrior you have become.
Do not succumb to vanity violence, please.

Have we not learned violence is bred by passion:
      passion that begets mental chaos:
      chaos breeding worldly strife?'

'We fought off demons yet from within
      it seems we are now evicted by a demon!'
'Our mother raises her head
      and you would shed your skin of her?'

'I'll be the fate that seats the right man
right on the throne an old man will leave cursed.'

'Dear Lakshmana, brother, our fate – it changes constant,
      it is always needing overwriting.
Would you turn the ground
by making Ayodhya a smoking graveyard? By pitching
      brother against brother? Dharma
is pure duty. What is life if life is without sacrifice?'

Lakshmana was fierce in riposte again, 'What life
if our actions do not create boundaries?
Are we not born noble to set limits?'

      'A man's character,
founded on fidelity and in debate with empathy,
shows if he is low grade or if he is truly high grade,
never the marble or straw under which he is born.'

Rama ran his fingers through Lakshmana's long hair
but the latter remained brow-knitted, saying,
'Why would you be a flame doused by a splash?'

'One fine thought makes more light than bare fire.'

'So in all our wandering with the great sage
have we not learned injustice flames the heavens
and the earth? Must we not make our own dharma
as the soul inherits and nurtures it from birth to birth?'

Slightly impatient, Rama said, 'Raavana too despises dharma.
So much mastery we have acquired from our sage
that now comes our chief test
and you would lash outwards dashing hard-won experience?'
'I would not a brass-neck usurper serve.'

'My dear Lakshmana, I believe Bharat and our mother, Kaikey,
        merit the throne.
Before we were even conceived
Bharat's mother saved our father from death.
Has she not been meted in kind? I was rash
claiming the throne. It is not the river's fault the bed is dry
no more is it the king's fault I will not be king.'

Their rift in the garden scattered under the rising sun
till Lakshmana said, 'I accept your course, Rama.
But my opinion keeps on its own route.'

'Whilst I am away, would you lead

matters here by supporting our mothers?'
'This bow is no ornament, this sword no decoration.
In your exile, every beast will zoom
    its beady
eye
upon your new career. I must follow
into that crucible.' Rama felt compelled to concede.

    And what of Sita?
Rama had assumed she'd remain dwelling in silk.

Sita had been up early assisting her mother-in-law, Kausalya,
with morning prayers. Then there she was in the courtyard

stripped from fancy face paints and jewels
(save for the Choodamani in her hair)
and saying to Rama, 'This bark cloth
    is fitting for the rains.
It shall be my raiment of renouncement.'

As in every Ramayana ever
Sita throws herself into the forest. It is her darn fate!

And in every Ramayana, Rama must always be trying
    to turn Sita from her kismet,

'Crookedly go the serpents across streams seeking prey . . .
fever soups the air . . . unhinged birds connive
from black trees . . .'

The Marriage Bow

Sita, always unimpressed,
whilst in Rama's grasp, saying, 'My Lord, I long
to view creatures only imagined . . . and flowers so fine
they swirl and rope towards heaven becoming finer than silk . . .
With you at my side water will be nectar, thistles silk.'

Dressed-down Sita set for the rocky ride.
Rama amorous for his warrior fellow.

Chapter Eight: Golden Slipper Nandigram Government

Bharat and Rama discuss who should be king.

~

O nce on the borders of the forest
  Rama looked at Ayodhya, pleading aloud,
'O finest jewel among cities!
O gods, I have done as you please –
may you grant me the justice
that I end my penance in the forest and embrace
    all my family again.'

Bharat missed his death-ferried father
but was bang on time for the burial
and for his appointment with kingly fate.
              The world was his
              and the world streamed
about his feet.

But what's this? No lover of lip service is baddie Bharat?
The astrological gossip-mongers

had to ditch their plottings when the new king abandoned
Ayodhya!
He was all horse hooves and hot on the tracks of Rama.

Rama had entered the woods when he was caught
by Bharat who was with his flying flags and army formation.
Lakshmana was ready
    for a right royal family-feud fisticuffs.

Rama pulled him back

then greeted Bharat, learning that their father died
a day after Rama had departed. Said Bharat,

'O Rama, what has befallen us?
    The mighty reign of our father
    might be remembered only
    for its sad end.

My mother's kingdoms of the air

    I have cast them all down before her

and blown away
    her two baleful wishes.

I feel awful, Rama.
I told my mother that when she favoured one son
    she lost all her sons.'

Bharat fell at Rama's feet
    and wept like a young elephant
newly captured. Rama calmly said,

'Weep not, dear King.
You must return to honour our father's wish.'

But Bharat's riposte was filled with his heart,
'Rama was born for the highest love, born to rule.'

Rama, now looking moved, said,
'You never desired such majesty
but you must bear the import of the role.
You must rise up becoming king over men.
I will rule over beasts in the great forest.'

'When a father has done wrong
the son must put him right.' But Rama's reply was,

'Bharat, a man's word is like a bowl of clear glass,
once broken – who can put back that bowl?
        That water?

Let us live the lives assigned us by our father.
That becomes our right. Or what is a father's word?
Should he be remembered by what the sons achieved
whilst bludgeoning his name with hot water?

Our twin brothers, so alike in their supporting natures,
will help us.

Satroogna with you in the palace
and Lakshmana with me in the forest.
Let us live the duty.'

'Would you lose it all, Rama? How I grieve for you.
When you, when Sita, when Lakshmana return
after fourteen heat-perishing years
can you be bold as you are today?'

A herd of gaur, with their heads of the bull
and their rumps of a lion, were heard treading nearby.

Rama was undistracted,
'My beautiful Bharat, like a stream never reverses its course
so our lives must accumulate till all the days
we have lived
surge, overwhelming, against our final
term.

I fear it is apt
this skin should weather and wrinkle, this hair
become blind to its boyhood. Our flesh is our daily psalm.

What can we do to Time when depletion reigns
upon unions by separation, as life by death?
As the ripe fruit falls about us
so it falls to us . . .

Each man's final night, when it passes: sooner curfew
the world of light

than summon a miracle to summon the touch of yesterday.

O my precious Bharat,
grieve for yourself. Why grieve for aught else?

All we can taste in our brief slot
    is each hour which remains immortal
if we flow along the right course, the kindred line.'

Bharat adding, 'May we all acquire the look
and the wisdom of age befitting kingship . . .'

In their sad to-and-fro, many complex arguments
    balanced on each side
amidst the gathered sages, elders and advisers.

The brothers contested rivalries over possession,
authority and borders. Each would end their point
with 'ours' or 'yours', never 'mine'.
Each conferring on the other a rightful throne.
Or rebutting with, 'So be it, if I have the authority
then I confer supreme power upon you.'

Throughout, Rama referred to Bharat's mother
in the kindest terms and always as 'mummy-jee'.
Lakshmana remained red-faced with rancour.

Even when their youngest brother, Satroogna,
with gold bracelets on his dark arms, brought Mantara
by her hair for punishment, Bharat forgave her,

appreciating instead her loyalty to Kaikey.
Then the brothers discussed the value of loyalty.

The gods watched the protracted public debate,
afraid that if Rama returned to the kingdom,
as was the wish of the peoples,
his authority would be weakened for reneging
the banishment as established by his father.

Sage Viswamithra heard all then intervened
that Bharat must rule for the full fourteen years.
Bharat was so impressed by Rama's integrity, he said,

'But not a day longer. How could I outlive my welcome?
        If you, Rama, do not appear
        when my time has passed

        I shall immolate myself.'

The gathering gasped. Bharat said he would rule
from Nandigram, a village on the outskirts of Ayodhya.
'I have before me these gold ornamented sandals.
        Please touch them, brother.'

Rama placed a cool palm upon the sandals.
Said Bharat. 'I shall raise these sandals
        upon the throne.
They will signal to the world,
from their place at the helm, that they are symbols
        of your power.

They will serve till your hands remove them
and place them on your feet
    that day your return king.'

Brothers all hugged and parted brothers.

      Lakshmana left praying,
      'Let no man by man be cast asunder.'

Book Third: Spick-Span Sylvan Exile

~

Chapter Two: At the Lord's Service

Raavana is holding court when . . .

~

L ord of the Underworld
(and many worlds beside)
is sitting on his somewhat overly encrusted throne
alongside his famed yaaal, with its six strings
plucked most tastefully from his own nerves.
Raavana, with his songs for Shiva:
> the god of strum and croon!

After morning's briefings and meetings
the lord is bantering with ne'er-do-well hangers-on
and hardcore bad guys including assassins, ghazis, nabobs,
riff-raff doolallys, famed hunger strikers and equality-wallahs,
> and amidst this miscellany dwell saintly raksassy
for the lord loves all who is loving his mandate of bliss.

To Vishnu well-wishers – this zone, what a stink:
in terms of music, say, the sounds are cacophonic,
in terms of fashion the ladies brag scrunch hair –

splatting the glare-eyes with mascara
> and adorning torn low-neck rags.

In terms of teeth, the ladies varnish
their teeth black as sapphire or egg-plant purple,
who but holy-molies have stained-white dentures!

Worst of all for Vishnu well-wishers –
ample boozy brain-idle womankind
are snogging stubbly men or baldly kissing fellow ladies.

Not nectars flowing from jewelled vessels
but flowing instead liquors made from fruits
jamming the head with no hangover. Drunkenness
is lasting days in non-stop laughs or sordid boomshakalaka!
Shonky conduct, indeed, in terms of Vishnu well-wishers.

Stooping amidst the veggie banquets, the ganja and liquor
are kings
whose kingdoms been won by the lord
and who the lord has condemned to servility.
They are bent-headed before him
with their hands upraised in prayer
and holding this position when on show
for fear any moment the lord might be thinking:
> *They is not enough servile*
> *I will crunch them now with a look!*

Specialist servants are full-time directed at the lord
> so if he make a command

they can finger-click to fulfil his want.

Black dahlia petals, upon the lord, are falling
and Wind-God, Vayu,   is routine returning
to puff away the curled petals.

Other divines at the service of the lord:
Dead-God, Yama, every hour gonging the time
and reporting how many mortals
        in the past hour he has killed
        (hooting only meets his hourly piece-rate,
        no wonder he feels loved here!)
Sun-God, Surya, keeps all lamps and incense lit
whilst Moon-God, Chandra, is delighting the gardens.

Most gods are serving the lord in person whilst some
are happy sending ministers: Fire-God has indulged a junior
to heat stoves for yummiest pulses and gourds
and Water-God's minister is being cheered en masse
each time he is nourishing the parched vats with wine.

        Lord of the Underworld,
with his twenty eyes, is ever watching circumambient.
His ten heads beaming their tamarind smile,
his ten heads from a distance are dog-ugly indeed
for who on two shoulders wears ten heads?
        CLOSE SHOT
and each face is film-star sexy
and with fangs projecting from his mouths
the madams all pun him, flatteringly of course,

Horny Boy!

Into this
      partying and general mela
      with no guilt and no harm taken
      or self-reflection next morning,
runs Raavana's
      one beloved sister
             Soorpanaka
                    caterwauling.

To which booms ten-headed Raavana,
'BASTARRDDDDS YOOOO ALLL SHUTTTING UPPPP.'
In a decahedron out-of-tune chorus
      at the sight of his even more tuneless kid sister.

Soorpanaka's panic has been so terror accosting
      that raksassy from the city
      have been road-rushing to witness
a face flattened woman wailing for the lord's pad.

Raavana, so shocked, spitting,

'What the bastard matter is with your face, sister?
What fucker-mother-bastard fuck with you, sister?'

Chapter Minus Two: Lollipop Ogre

Rama, Sita and Lakshmana meet a dweller of the forest.

⁓

The undulatingly gharam sun across Dandaka forest.
And across it moving deeper and darker onward
seduced by sandalwood and suchlike aromas,
onward for a homestead
through the trackless red-burr bushes and brush . . .

Such trees they never before had seen
for the trees were wrapped fiercely around by creepers,
　　　creepers sucking each tree's squinge-breath.

The lakes deep and the water still as slate, chilled.
　　　　　The birds phlegm-barking
whilst that sly blood-eyed cuckoo, the kokila, snuck its

eggs. Said Rama, 'I hear a breath – is it poised to pounce?'
　　　　　　　　　　　　'I am ready to
pounce back!' added Lakshmana.

They were standing before
    a giant-as-trees fellow with a headless torso.
    His mouth was on his belly
and above the belly-head, a sole yellow eye.

The ogre was dressed in bloodied
tiger-skins sloppily patched. Poor stitchwork. In its hand
a pole
impaled with heads from two
    wolves, three tigers and four lions!
    The heads were
    crammed on the top
    like a juicy
    but a bit drippy
    lollipop.

The ogre licked the warm blood
    with the tongue on his belly.
Knowing the onlookers would take a while
    taking in his pell-mell

the beast had already pounced at Sita
    and stuffed her under his spare arm.
Sita shrieked as she eye-ball'd
the dead heads in the monster's other hand
and eye-ball'd the monster's forehead winking-eye.

Monster to Sita, 'You is beautipul. Beautipul!'

Then to amuse himself with the boys,

'What, I, some huckster, hawker-wallah,
selling my drippy caboodle, you think? Not for sale!
You humans with matted hair is not in priest dress.
Who is you, with this rundy-randy?'

Rama was struck with shock so the ogre continued,
'I am Viradha, a gandharva. We, my kind
        dinner on raw, even cooked, man.'

The boys kept still for fear Sita might be killed.
'I will make this rundy-randy my bride.
If you do not scram I will be drinking your blood
        at our wedding service.'

Viradha bounded away with Sita. Sita begging,
'Spare the princes. Drink only me.'
But Viradha was a cheeky gandharva, 'I will be
drinking you too in darling lovemaking!'

Running after Viradha, the brothers shot arrows that
        stuck in his back – porcupining him.
Tickled by these irritants, Viradha turned around,

'I was granted a boon that I not be killed by weapons.
How you cubs kill me
        with your girly figures?'

He dropped Sita to the floor and ran at the brothers.
Rama shot an arrow that split Viradha's trident.
Viradha pulled out a sword
        and the boys sword-fought Viradha.

Viradha was getting overwhelmed
by the virtuoso sword skills of the mortals.
He was impressed; so impressed he ran away.

But the boys were at him. They grabbed him
and sliced off
his arms. Viradha squirmed on the ground.

They punched him up pretty bad. Viradha was blood-guts.
        But still breathing.
Lakshmana was trying to cease the squirming
so he could stab the eye in the ogre's chest.

Viradha whined, 'Who is you two, so hardcore?'

When he heard the name Rama, his soggy mouth said,
'I was told by Wealth-God, Kubera, I only shed this
tortured body should I die at Rama's hands,
this Rama who is gifted with worldly riches
that the sound of his name

                miracles rebirth.'

Rama was flattered into perplexity, and enquired,
'If you once lived in the heavens
        how did you come into this . . . ?'

'I was cut to this form for being an upstart
        who is so cheeky

that the great artist Ramba is happy
        bedding him!

Kubera getting irked by my upstarting
cursed me so I became this poor monster.
I'm pleading, you bury me in a very deep pit.'

The boys questioned Viradha further
then after digging a pit filled it with Viradha bits.
They could hear Viradha's soiled gross-glee,

'This sick frame in a sick life . . .
      I must again be worth . . . heaven!'

The brothers stood perplexed, but saluted one whose soul
evacuated eagerly
                from its mocked
                life – careering
                in an upwards
                bromine haze.

Chapter Minus One.five: Until Mahanirodhanibbana

Rama and Sita argue about the use of force.

~

' . . . must you have come to the forest, Sita?
All about us, we are crowded by cruel hootings,'
said Rama, still spattered with Viradha's blood.

But Sita, who had started the tiff, was sleeves up-rolled,
'Rama, you will become hardened by all these killings.
Could guile or prayers not support us in this forest?'
'Our warrior conduct insists I put out demons.'

Sita was calm, 'Dharma demands relenting
one's violence potential at all times. Do you need to cut off
quite so many limbs in the name of killing?'

'I must send out a message to the forest demons.'

'Should not war be properly justified?
You would not a falsehood utter,
nor, I know, you would not wrongly touch

another woman, so I assume you would fight
according to proper provokings and limits.'

'But Sita, these raksassy, gandharva and arsoora
    do not fight by our rules.'

Sita softening, 'I sense our caste duty
is to destroy evil just as I sense
    dry fuel bursts into flame when near a fire,
and that a warrior is ignited by a blade at hand.
Let me tell you a short tale, please, Rama?'

They sat cuddly against a branch as Sita spoke,
'Long ago a sage who lived among birds and fruits
had his limit tested by the god, Indra.
One day the god changed into a soldier
carrying a sword. On his way to an ashram,
    he left his sword with the sage.

At first the sage merely admired the studded sword
but soon the bright blade was like a temptress.
He said to himself, "What fine execution this will do
    if in mighty hands."

First he was merely touching it to feel its weight
then soon enough he found himself
                  chopping from high trees
bright fruits. Then soon carrying it willy-nilly.

When Indra returned to collect his sword

he saw, to his horror, all about the sage's hermitage
     a carcass gallery. Motley dead animals
whose throats had been cut in a spree
        lay scattered about this once veggie.

    Flies, guts and blood ubiquitous.

Indra was so scorned by the sage's butchered
lusting soul
      he sent him ek-dum

      into the underworld!

Rama, perhaps your bow wielding
will shield your feelings from a lover's slight
touch . . .'

'Indeed, Sita, how wise are you.
I must always keep a pure mind up
albeit I must clean from this kingdom barbarity.'

'I wish you will not interfere in every forest dispute.'

Rama looked towards the dozing heavens and said,
'I promise, Sita, one day we will live
in that sphere where we are free as spirits,
free without bonds and attachments in that place known as

    Mahanirodhanibbana.'

Sita smiled as she followed Rama
to their makeshift abode;
    Sita carrying his bow and arrow.

Chapter Zero.one: The Goat Cannibal Killer!

A sage explains his recent conduct in dealing with two demons.

~

They went south and arrived at an ashram
to meet the . . . the great Sage Agastya.
It's said if all the sagacity and spiritual penance between
the Himalayas and Vindhyas were placed on one scale
and Agastya on the other, the northern scale
would be tossed
    upwards by his weight!

The sage looked tortured,
'. . . a colony of us sages live nearby
and your fourteen-year tour in our midst
may support us but lately we been losing ourselves.

Rama, all type demons recently infested-pested
    this formerly peaceful forest,
they rub their chummy-tummy
at the thought of eating sages dead raw.

I tell you Rama, if we sages were not bent upon pure peace
neither could the world survive our wrath
nor a single demon survive our slaying-playing.

But I had had enough of peace, I tell you!
To my shame, I lately ended a foul caper-shaper.
Too many sages have been wiped out
and we have been under threat for our lives.

I learned about a mad-bad goat business.
Two raksassy become fatty-boys on eating sages.
One raksassy, Ilvala, will pretend he is a sage
and then as a pretend-sage he befriends a real sage.
The other raksassy, Vatapi, will then show up
     as a goat, as a bleating goat.

The sage and his new friend, Ilvala, will kill this goat
     for jolly good din-dins.

When the goat has filled the bellies of the new chums
Ilvala will then suddenly bawl,
"Out now you please come, Vatapi, matey!"

At this racket-packet, the real sage
hears a bleating from his stomach
and then a hot feeling and straight his tummy
will rip a snip.
Before he knows it
     his guts
will be stripped apart like two curtains pulled back

to unveil the actor:
he who was once a goat now becomes Vatapi again.

The dead sage is then din-dins for Ilvala and Vatapi.
Drat chum-buddy Dinnertime, I call it.
So what I do? I chucked in my praying.

I chucked it in and sought Vatapi.
When I found him I followed his pitter-patter:
O look, there is a gorgeous goat, he said,
why don't we chase it . . . O let's kill it . . .
Suchlike bunkum-pocus I "yes, yes, good idea" agreed upon
then we killed it, skewered it, cooked it.

Said Ilvala, "Not too much we cook it,
    I like juicy meat,"
but already I burnt the goat a bit.

Then we were biting-shiting goat meat.
I chewed each shitey-bitey over hundred times.

Irked, Ilvala finally tried to rend me,
"Out now you please come, Vatapi, matey!"
He thought he'd make good din-dins with my doughty figure.
But no! No, no gut cutting I felt.
Nor no tummy burst or even split in my inner lining.
The risk I ran paid off. I had eaten Vatapi
    a bit too pukka.

Not off-guard was I caught. I mocked Ilvala,
"What is it, my gut catch your matey's tongue?"

He switched from benignant old sage to raksassy
with long poison claws ready-steady for me.

> Till I looked him in the eyes
> and with my red-flame look
> I chewed him fine
> into dust
> powdering
> upon a dry

leaf.'

The gutsy Agastya, ashamed of his own 'warrior' tale,
was consoled by Rama, 'Peace is not on high.
> It must be grafted with soiled hands.'

'My dear Rama, I am breaching the word,
dharma, daiva, karma and so on so.
I must recover my former powers – beginning again
> penance.'

Rama kneeled, saying,
'We will pray for you. Then we must move deeper
for we are still too close to the forest borders.'

Chapter Zero.zero: Dear Diary

Sita writes about their new home.

~

'. . . then once roaming under the nyagrodha trees what a feeling of watery coolness within the shade. Rama said these nyagrodhas are famed for housing a thousand elephants beneath their unending expanse. The forest is protection and primitive pain, for sure.

Even the vultures are primordial here. We sighted one such giant on a branch. It said, "Lord Rama, I was your father's companion once and we were so close you will have heard it remarked: if King Dasaratha equals body then Jatayu equals soul to total a whole."

Having been recently roughly touched about by poor tormented Viradha Jatayu's calmness was good for my nerves! Jatayu glows from good feeds on ogre meals, and with his voice cut-glass he is excellently dashing.

What comfort he has served us. He said, "My Lord, you are imperilled here. Follow in my wide shading wings and I will take you to a safe life in Panchavati. It is a dark grove mingled with flame trees, trees safe from forest fires. Nearby, you will find plantain trees with their dessert banana; near too and fast growing the finest rice since its bright seeds are sharp-tipped."

After days, and a huge distance south from Ayodhya we arrived by the Godavari river, in Panchavati. We were struck by the stream wafting perfumes from the lotus and the grounds strewn with dharba grass for our garments. Rama used a word from his region, 'cushy' which he told me means 'joyous', then embracing me

he said, "How cushy I am Sita! How cushy you are always making me, always my Sita; and how cushy is the bounteous giving Godavari, and how cushy are the deer in their freedom roaming, and cushy too are the peacocks by the mountains whilst glowing crimson in tippy-tappy dance about the flowering cashew!"

Rama and I went cushy along the river, knowing full well our dear Lakshmana will have already killed a blackbuck for its meat and brought lotuses from the calm verges. We then made meat and flower offerings and prayers. Within days, at the tableland of rills, by a clear spring, Lakshmana had beautifully brought materials from our midst and built a solid house that was framed with long bamboos and floored with grass. He wove the walls with chunky wood which he tightly lashed to keep the wind out. I watched him applying clay, like an artist at fast and efficient work. Like a seamstress with sequins, to dazzle our abode, Lakshmana laid peacock feathers intimately, one over the other. Then he took some wood ribbons and latched them over the feathers to secure the iridescent colours, which like a thatch, or a lit crown, became our roof. Rama simply hugged his Lakshmana. Lakshmana looking shy, "Such work is reward enough."

What a blessing if we could live in peace treasured 'midst our banana plantations, with honey from the hives whilst spearing beasts for their scrumptious meat. Oh and also dealing easily with the odd demon who is dropping by!

Fourteen years spent quietly, uneventfully, meditating . . . Could there be a blessing, a greater blessing than this exile sweet exile, in our spick-span sylvan luxury!'

Chapter One: Meet the tad Nuts Neighbour

A woman approaches Rama.

~

Curvaceous succulent beautification's copper-hair-tossing
mesmeric damsel with eyes sparkling
and smacking hot lips plus bursting-out
    bounteous yet conically chiselled chest-smackers!
Also with anklets jingling for a teeny
    orchestra accompanying those pamper-grass sways.
        Whose slender frame
           was like a golden creeper
           that climbs up
              the kalpak tree
                for the seventh

                            orgiastic

        heaven . . .

Late one evening, in the thirteenth year
of their uneventful life in the forest,
amidst the creepers and plants in the front yard
Rama saw real/unreal

multitudinous perched cobra heads in gaps, on branches
    near or far glinting in a hissing crucible

ssssssssssssssss ssssssssssssssssssssssssssssssssssssssssssssss sss
sssssssssssssssssssss sssssssssssssssssssssssss sssssssssssssssss
ssssssss sssssssssssssssssssssssssssssss ssssssssssssssssssssssssss

    but all vanished as Rama saw glowing in their place
    a lady comparable, perhaps, even to Sita
    at the garden gate.

Said Rama 'Namastey, dear one. What
    brings you visiting us?
    May I ask precisely who you are?'
Could this be a heretic disguised as an ascetic . . .

'My name is Soorpanaka.' What a bass voice!
'I am meagred by confessing my big brother is . . . Raavana.'

Not meaning to be rude, Rama asked,
'If you are Raavana's sister
how is it you have acquired such a perfect form?'

'I mimic our brother, Vibishana:
I too repel sin, giving victory cup only to goodliness.
I ripped into my fitness figure through awesome praying.'

Rama was wowed. But quick back into his thoughts,
'If you are sister to Lord of the Underworld
where are your attendants? Your bearers?

You parade about unescorted?'

'Pageantry is but dry papaya in the throat.
     I stand before you with a view in mind.
It would be crude for a lady of my pureness
          to unmask my smooching mission . . .'

But unmask it all straightaway she did,

'I'm opened by Love-God. Only yester-morn
for the first time I see it:
          your moist blue
          lissom blue build.
Your aura or charisma disembowelling me giddy,
not before am I feeling weak as a frond . . .'
Rama watched her blush. He remained silent.

'Not knowing you are basking beautiful in my demesne,
how much life I toiled by kissing holy feet.
Now I have peeled you from behind these trees
my womanhood can be imminent unbusted.
My slurpy idle mud-ridden life is now
          heading for the blue.'

Rama pitied that blushing malarkey damsel.
Not wanting to seem austere, 'I am from the keshatriya race . . .
and you are raksassy. Our alliance is inconceivable.'

'I'm humbly saying I'm unharnessed from my brother.
I'm seeking only fellowship with good-eggs.'

Then with deep impatient breath, in, she plunged.
    'O you with the Vishnu lookliness!

If only we

marry – my brothers will unratchet their hatred
        for your race.

They will bless you with overlordship of multiple worlds.
O Rama, I imagine you and me grafting together!'

Rama was amused by this stunner,
'So the fruits of my penance and sacrifices
        are to be blessed by a pack of demons . . .
    I should trade my soul's strengthening
for hedonistic dark sarcastic artistry . . . ?'

Soorpanaka distracted . . .
        What? What's this?
Long leg walker, by nature?

In every way hot as my totty-hotness???

Soorpanaka struck by a lady coming out from the cottage.
Soorpanaka's mouth open
                as though she had bitten
                        hot meat.

'Who is this?' asked Sita.

Soorpanaka watched effulgent peach-light
porched at Sita's feet and whirling about her till it peaked
      in a teeny halo above her head.

Poor Soorpanaka realised if this bedfellow
were Rama's, she had no chance.
She watched the pair in chat – a perfect couple.

Perfect man with woman, also perfect. All so perfect.
Soorpanaka in a spell. Thinking to herself: surely
she is beauty that remains memorable in our hearts,
that has no flaw beyond its creator's flaws . . .
If my eyes cannot leave her
      how she must be famishing each beholder . . .

Saddened Soorpanaka decided this could not be Rama's wife
for what wife would rough it: palace or forest,
who would choose a life picking sticks and stones
when what could be had
      were servants and divans on marble floors.

He must have a wife back home . . .
This must be his fair dinkum on the side . . .
Rama's roguery, as imagined by Soorpanaka,
titillated and fondled further her Rama feelings.

Sharp as a brick, Soorpanaka butted in at the perfect couple,
'Great one, don't let this lady put your face in a spin!
      She is some raksassy for sure.
      It takes one to know one!'

Soorpanaka's base bitch-licks hit a stonewall silence.
She changed tack, 'Dear girl, please leaving alone
me and my beloved. We are in bona fide courtship.'

Sita turned red at hearing this odd chat.
Rama replied, 'Dear Soorpanaka, it would please us greatly
if you departed back to your sage's hermitage.'

Rama shut the cottage door.

Chapter One & Half: The Crazy Chukar

Lovesick Soorpanaka plans to win Rama.

~

What a cuss – a door shut in your face!
Really, to Soorpanaka it had never before happened.
Who dare shut the door on her and still be room-roaming?
That's how awful could be her bad-breath wrath.

This was sad-eyed Soorpanaka.
No curvaceous succulent hotty on a par with Sita.
Not at all, in reality sad Soorpanaka
had lunatic's matted hair,
flame-coloured fangs with birth-black teeth,
a brass-pot belly from all the rodent and fowl she eat.
Here's a rat – shove it home, ummm what a salty tail;
here's a cat – in one juicy bite, fur and all, get it down, dearie!
And so on all damn tubby day long.

Raavana had given his kid sister
the whole Dandaka forest
as her own domain to dominate every which way,

she was assisted by several heartless demons
including one of her brothers, Kora: terse horsey-face.

Soorpanaka, for the first time ever had chanced upon
     vulnerability.
To satisfy vulnerabilities calling she had herself
changed into a comely maiden to win Rama.
But for what?   Door in the face treatment.

In her new fit figure she faffed around eating
     more rodents than ever before.
For a laugh she bit off a cow's tail or a pig's foot
leaving the cow untailed, the pig three-trotted and tragic.

She entered the emotional landscape
     of all race and caste adhering mortals:
dreamy passivity for the lover your folks not pick for you!

Sickened by her own forest and sickening for Rama
she shut herself in a cave that was
     infested with a carpet of deadly serpents.
     She writhed amidst their darkness writhing.
In dreams, Rama mastered her – pinned her to a rock and
slapped her
biting her lips and bending back her legs . . .

After the exhausted hours, she awoke
(to the great relief of the serpents).
Fresh energy on fresh hope at winning Rama.

Back at the Godavari river and spying,
she watched Rama blitz the surface with his powered strokes.
Soorpanaka watched and thought again,
what a dish! What a sizzling fillet!
As Rama swam away, she dashed to Rama's cottage
and saw Sita gathering flowers from the garden.

Soorpanaka imagined that if she stole, and perhaps consumed,
this gorgeous morsel before her,
Rama might in time forget losing Sita,
and soon he might sift the forest for a fresh bit on the side.
And **ta-dah!** there she'd be . . .

Soorpanaka leapt on Sita to grab her away.
To Sita, this comely woman was unusually powerful
        for Sita was lifted off the ground
        and swept out the garden.

But what is this? *Not so fastly missus floozie* . . .
        Lakshmana had been posted behind a shaded eminence
        ever-alert to a foul deed.

Soorpanaka was dragging Sita out into the thick
        when Lakshmana leapt before the pair.
Soorpanaka became impolite towards Lakshmana.

His hot-head was NOT motivated to kindness
when Soorpanaka started accusing him of
        incest, sodomy, paedophilia and so on . . .

Lakshmana took out his sword with a whip speed

    and sliced off

Soorpanaka's   perfect   nose
                                    ears
                                    nipples!

Soorpanaka watched her bits about the ground.
Shocked at Lakshmana's swordplay
    she ran off cursing the skies:
how dare a mortal flatten her frontage.
How dare he do it to Raavana's sister!

She reached her chariot and came across Rama,
to his q & a she spoke in kind.

He: 'What has happened? Why are you
in such a bloody state? Who are you?
She: 'Do you not know me? Do you not
remember our courtship last night?' Even now
    will you not protect me, my Lord?

He: 'Are you who I think you are?'
She: 'Arrey, yes, why must you forget me?'

Rama recognised her and withered.
Soorpanaka humiliated at being, in this bodged state, watched.

Love's folly, whilst she clutched at leaves
    to cease her bloody shame
still no less emboldened was her ardour for Rama.

    Her only hurt: heart-ache for him.

She begged, 'My Lord, I can instruct you in our arts,
the magic and suchlike that make my race mighty.
I will help you defeat raksassy. My brother
will grow me back more ears, nose, nipples!'

Rama looked away.

Soorpanaka pleaded again, 'O Rama
even now if you take me, Raavana will forgive all.
    Or for this cut-cut-cutting
he will mess up all mankind. All raksassy
    will go mad about earth
cleansing it free of humanity! Torture, slaughter,
genocide and suchlike are piffle words
    to their mankind clean out.'

'I think it best you return to your kind.
I will deal with them one by one or all as one.'

Just as the Chukar Partridge, from its promontory,
stares at the awesome heart of the moon
    and cannot help
but stare at the heart till she's dizzied by the gaze

and still the moon will remain stone-faced
     in the face of her awful suffering
so too, even now, whilst staring at Rama
Soorpanaka felt brutal tears
     like moon-lumps upon her cheeks
woozying her. How she loved Rama;
would die for Rama; he gave her no heart.

Chapter Three: Sexing Big Bro

Soorpanaka tells Raavana about Rama and Sita.

~

'BASTARRDDDDS YOOOO ALLL SHUTTTING UPPP.'
Boomed Raavana in a decahedron out-of-tune chorus
at the sight of his even more tuneless kid sister.

'What the bastard matter is with your face, sister?
What fucker-mother-bastard fuck with you, sister?'

Soorpanaka had been repaired by the magicians
but was still hurting inside. She approached her brother
who was raving, 'Your nipples been cut. Your nipples!
        Cut too your nose.
Who so mad would stake his honour?'
'O brother, how come you have no broadcast
about newcomers to Dandaka!?'
'Why sister, it is your domain to dominate.'
Replied Soorpanaka, 'These brothers seem cosy with customs
yet are resident in our woods and eyeing for a fight.'

'They have poked their finger in a black snake's eye!'

'One man, Rama, is beautifully limbed and lotus eyed.
His swimming, archery and swordplay are a parable, his —'
'Adulation? In dishonour? For a holy-moly!'

She changed the mood, 'By their side
the hot-most paragon I ever laid my star-struck eyes on.
          I swear she have torpedo chest
                    bombasticating through her rustic robes!'

Kora, the fiercest, was tense and terse as ever,
'Death kill them all. All man dead.
Shall I get them and boil man-mince vats now, Lord?'

Raavana looked distracted, to Soorpanaka,
'Draw this woman's image.'
'Even if I had amplitude tongues I could not enliven
this man's hotness. His speaking is music . . .'
'Can you not hold your senses from drawing him?'

Soorpanaka, still hankering for Rama, tried anew
to win him . . . She dreamt of Raavana with Sita
and herself with Rama. To arrange the marriage

          she gently scratched
          slow fine black lines across the page
          for Sita's face and
          tantalising body entire.

The completed sketch matched so perfectly its subject
that it seemed to enter a godliness glow. The glow

like a wound grew and wore

into Raavana's lust.

Raavana weakly heard Soorpanaka,
'Even if I had amplitude tongues
I could not enliven this famed, this voguery-glamoury
        lady's hot-babe-ness whose name
            even the leaves sing swishingly . . .
Or I cannot enliven enough her legs robust and sinuous
            like elephant trunks
or her red-hot caressing smile. Or the banana whiffery
deep in her pits.'

Raavana, gobsmacked, 'I need to compare her.'

When Raavana regained himself from the portrait
he plotted a way to compare her. To execute the plot
he sought his uncle, Mareecha,
        and found him buried in prayer.

Mareecha, as ever, was repenting his wild youth:
along with his brother he had rampaged
around a desert created by his mother, Tadaka.

Said Raavana, 'Uncle, pray not to the gods,
they must be laughing at us for the insult to Soorpanaka
by a mortal who is remaining unrevenged.
He should be taxed in pain,
    taxed to the ends of his shame.'

Said Mareecha, 'I hear his name is Rama.
We should just let him live out his mere mortal term.'
'You must break this fast and support me, Uncle.'
Raavana sat on the floor next to Mareecha and heard,

'I once felt the arm of this Rama. He broke a great bow.'
Raavana reacted, 'And what of it? I shook Shiva's abode,
    Mount Kailas itself.'

'I watched this Rama without strain
kill my mighty mother.'

Raavana, usually so charismatic, again reacted,
'I am not requesting you tell me what is good or bad here,
or who may or may not be mustering much vim.
Only I am requesting a piece of service,
and forget not how I am providing you the fortune
    of winning revenge.'

Mareecha, almost mumbling,
'In this world it happens time and time again,
one man is deafening and thousands feel the shock.
It is not the one who does not listen that alone suffers.'

Raavana interjected, 'How can this Sita,
famed for her beauty, desire a mere mortal?

Is it a blessing or a curse but every woman ever
has looked with love-heart candying eyes upon me.
These riches that Kubera endowed in my person
pull me beyond my mind's vast engine.'

Mareecha sounded wearied, 'This seems a gargantuan
flaw

                              leaving your heart
exposed.'

Whilst Raavana talked, Mareecha mused to himself
about the nine types of men, who if angered, cause ill;
the nine being the rich, the rogue, the spy, the soldier,
the priest, the doctor, the poet, the bard of the charmed voice
      and, of course, the ruler.

Raavana stood up
      and simply cheered himself,
'. . . so no more of this rhapsodising and pious mumbling.
          You only can help me Mareecha.
          Get Rama gallivanting for you
          and I the rest to his piety will do!'

Chapter Four: Golden Deer, please!

Sita sees a golden deer and wants to keep it.

~

A golden deer with precious stones
naturally bristling from its legs.

Wahwah, thought Sita whilst strolling around Panchavati.
Then rushing indoors to Rama,

'That animal over there followed me to our gate.
What silver streaming circles over its skin,
its hooves must be lapis lazuli. What high-grade gold.
    Could we keep it here?
Or if it is slippery to catch could we not keep
its skin for when we return to the palace?'

Lakshmana looking outside,

                              'See the other deer

are keeping back from it. Let it nibble away.

Surely no goldie creature lives.'

Said Rama, 'Vishnu's creations are endless and beauteous.
How can we know for sure
such a creature couldn't exist?'

Said Sita, 'If you two debate this till supper
the deer will run off
becoming once more illusion.'
They laughed at Sita's comic timing.

Lakshmana persevered it must be an 'infernal thing'
and, '. . . it could be Mareecha, the raksassy,
famed for changing into animals.
No end of hunting kings has this deer-demon killed for his
dinner.'

Rama's hunch was contrary.
He wanted so much to please his unpampered wife
and said to Sita,

'Your wishes are my duty.'

Then ran for the deer. The deer ran far off

but kept pricking its ears in a cheeky come-on,
and each time Rama nearly caught up,
the deer would draw its hooves to its ears
then spring
zigzagging away

to emerge on a hill
    with a passing cloud behind it.

How long had he chased the deer . . . ?
Lakshmana might be correct. Sighting the deer again,
    Rama shot an arrow,
shot an arrow direct into its comb-haired belly.

Mareecha, who all along had been the deer,
    and had been running
    at the speed of fear was slain.
Still he remembered to complete his mission,
and screamed out in Rama's voice,

'O Lakshmana!

O Sitaaaaa!

Help

meeeeeeeeeeeeeee!!!'

Rama deafened by the deer. The deer dying
was turning into saint, a saintly raksassy.
    Wholly improbable! Mareecha's cry

sped

    for Sita's ears.

            Sita flipped,

'Go Lakshmana.

      I heard Rama.
   He is surely hurt. O please, now, go!'

Sita sobbed at Lakshmana's protests,
'Don't you know your own husband?
Who could hurt him? Would Rama cry out?'

   Sita looked daggers at him,
      shouting *go!*

Lakshmana felt caught. He said, 'I will go
but on one condition.

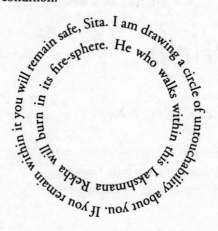

remain safe, Sita. I am drawing a circle of untouchability about you. He who walks within this Lakshmana Rekha will burn in its fire-sphere. If you remain within it you will

Jatayu must be close.'

'Go!!!'

Chapter Five: One Shot: Thirteen!

Rama and Lakshmana are surrounded by Mareecha's army.

~

Ambush extraordinary.
When Lakshmana caught up with Rama
and word ringed the woods that before reaching his army
     Mareecha had been killed
     Mareecha's army had near-ringed Rama.

Into this forest cauldron near bubbling with heat
fell Lakshmana. Two against two hundred at least.

Training from Sage Viswamithra must be employed, NOW.

Crimson streaked the sky. Rama smiled,
'You come at a charmed time.
I sense foul shapes behind hills and trees.'

Said Lakshmana, 'My right hand is throbbing,
look how my arrows fume and ooze smoke.'

The dead man's dear army came forth on sea monsters.
They beat their great gongs for battle. The battle began.
Hundreds of gold-tipped arrows
    like sun-rays danced towards the brothers.

The brothers jinked and funked

till each arrow was shielded or flunked away
        though one or two left them scorched.

Rama's bow was bent back
        on itself circumferencing
almost to a circle.
His heron-feathered arrow after arrow
blitzed the scene. The brother's arrows largely met flesh.

The cauldron was clogged with death cries.
Round after round beat back
    raksassy arrows and tridents.

Forth stepped the valiant Trishira who thundered his chariot
at Rama
then fired such a potent volley of arrows
that three landed in Rama's forehead
yet Rama called out,

    'This is being struck by flowers!'

Rama fought back with arrows. The two men's arrows
    met head to head and fell away.

Rama and Trishira now fought with swords. Their power
equivalent to that between a lion and an elephant in combat.

Trishira was no turn up for the books

eye-poker from the cradle

      he stabbed Rama in the chest!

This merely impressed Rama who admired a skilled fighter
and lamented the tragic waste of a craftsman turned rogue.

With sufficient wits
    Rama managed to counter so his blade
    went through Trishira's heart
    as a snake slips down an anthill.

Lakshmana's powerful arrow-rounds soon diminished
    the remaining soldiers.

    It was horsey-face Kora next,
Raavana's brother, who stepped forth in his chariot –

ornamented with refined gold, with poles made of beryl
and its sides carved with fish, flowers, moons and stars.

He punched his chariot through the skies
then struck arrows down at Rama,
    invincible arrows like sparkling fires,
    so many close-leaning arrows at once

that Rama was pierced.

Kora stormed for Rama

but Rama, streaking blood,
had the measure of Kora and with an almighty arrow

    he severed Kora's gold-notched standard
    bringing the craft to ground.

Rama fired off six selected arrows at Kora's head.
Kora slapped back the arrows with his own arrows.
Kora fired four arrows that tore at Rama's legs.

      Rama was now furious.

    ➤   ➤   ➤

      In his controlled fury,

➤ ➤ ➤ ➤ ➤ ➤

      he shot thirteen

    ➤   ➤   ➤

      whetted arrows!

      ➤

The arrows sliced through

Kora's thick-shouldered yoke with one,
his four horses with four,
the charioteer's head with the sixth,
three smashed the triple pole,
    two the axle,

Kora's bow and arrow with his twelfth arrow,
and the thirteenth,
the thunderbolt arrow, ripped all over the shop

    the floor-flooding Kora body.

Any soldiers still with hope
    now scrammed from the scene.
Scrammed from the scene
    of thirteen wowser arrows, by jiminy!

Chapter Six: How to simply Sweep a Lady off her Feet

An old man visits Sita whilst Lakshmana is away searching for Rama.

~

A rat-a-tat-tapping at the cottage entrance
　　at which the very trees held their breath.
The air. Did it move? No. Wind-God scarpered.

Nature's inner-turmoil at an elderly sage in ochre robes.
Even Avari, the River-God, flowed softly
　　　　for fear the sage send it off course
　　　　　　with a curse, from his mouth,
　　　　　　　　for no good reason popping out.

'Is anybody . . . there? Anybody . . . to welcome
　　　　an old but benignant sage?'
　　　　　　Trembly watery voice.
The sage was lean, holding a staff and begging bowl.

Sita had been praying for Rama when she answered the door.

At his first Sita-sight,
    the old man buzzing
abutting his own teeming blood.

Sita stood there: even in drab garb
    she looked a grab!

        She was a streak of lightning
        felling the crusty oldie.

He noticed her brows like the bow of a goddess,
the cups of her breasts propped
and proud as lotus buds
her skin clear as a jewel
and her complexion shining as if floating with gold.

This not being reward enough
the sage spoke his finest Sanskrit,
'Some alms for one who kindly always
prostrate prays for the correct three-world conduct?'

The old man watched Sita contemplate an offering.
    He saw too the faint golden circle
and knew it was a circle of untouchability,
    the Circle of Chastity.

He saw Sita remained inside it.
He wondered if he could tease her out of it.

'I cannot go to the kitchen so could you please

help yourself in there.'

'But madam, an alm is bestowed. Not taken.
    Am I looking a crook?'

'You must be a mighty sage to be so deep in the forest.'
'It is rumoured.' The old man, unbeknown to himself,
    blushed.

To obtain the rice grains
Sita must leave the Lakshmana Rekha.
Sita furrowed her forehead.

             She looked outside.

As if lost
      in a moment

when a moment is definitive

           Sita crossed

the threshold, the golden Rekha

and as she walked across it it

vanished . . . Sita watched
          her grains
          fill the old
          man's bowl.

The sage was already imagining
his impending life of Riley now the impediment was gone.
He thought to himself, I shall make her queen of my empire
and spend my life executing her cutie commands.
How amazing was my sister to spot the perfect lady.
I must make my sister the queen of my empire
whilst I go tooty-footing everyday with Sita . . .

He was already forgetting
Sita would be queen of his kingdom. Sita enquired,
'What brings a frail sage so deep in this forest?'

Somewhat swoony-mooded and smiley,
'I am here to adore the omniscient ultimate: the
      chuckerbutty.
He, with ten astounding heads, cornucopias life.
    Have you not felt the chuckerbutty?'

Sita felt bested; parched,
    'I had heard bad rumour.'

The old man thought he'd win her in his elderly state,
'Each lady he chucker, that is to say, walk around,
    he makes divine.'

'Is this chuckerbutty a raksassy?'

        Nothing hard to lean
    at, she stared
outside.

'Indeed, raksassy are the most blissed
but not lax as they are publicised.'

From somewhere hardening in herself,
'I think . . . their salad days are done.
My Lord's mission – to rid them; building peace . . .' 'No
meagre man can do that.
It would be like a rabbit goring an elephant gang.'
The old man was so close that he stank of tamarind.

'Did not once a mere two-shoulder man called Parasuram
once coop this mighty ten-headed Raavana
till he was weeping for release?' Sudden
the old man's blood shot up. He ground his teeth.

Like heaped snake skins
his wrinkly skin flaked off for the floor.

He expanded to his normal

freak finicky contours.
Sita was startled.

'Hello Lady,
now before you I am
the divine Raavana.

O swanlike one

my ten heads have never before bowed to another.
>   You are beauty's flame.'

He took off his crowns
>   dropped to his ten brows
>   and knelt before Sita.

Sita impassioned herself and –
'Do I look the touching kind?
My Lord's hands are now flying for your heart.'

Raavana liked her even more for the spirited attack.
'Rama's darts cannot catch me.
Sooner expect a mountain to split from a straw touch.'

Raavana was a true lover:
only careful wooing was the way he would float her boat.
But he felt rushed, it came out too cocky,
'Come now to my crystal bed in Lanka.
>   Let's be getting tip-top pleasure!'

Sita waxed back, enraged,
'What gulf there is between a lion and a jackal
>   there is between you and Rama.
What gulf there is between a nectar and sour gruel
>   there is between you and Rama.'
And on she could have gone comparing
gold and lead, elephant and cat, sandalwood and mire

EXCEPT that

rather than vilely grab Sita and cheapen her beauty,
Raavana, from under Sita's feet,

simply by the power of one gentle hand

> was scooping up
> the ground beneath her.

Sita was being lifted.

He carried the lot to his chariot which was powered by
> a tandem team of lions!
> A team of lions that flew vamooooooose . . .

Sita was still shouting, 'You goonda!' to Raavana

and at the heavens, **'BACHAO ! ! !'**

Poor old tired sleepy Jatayu

> heard screams above his tree.

He flew out and was soon out there wide awake
alongside Raavana, saying,

> 'You are a famous king,
perhaps even the god of all gods.

Many have called you the ten-peaked King of Heaven.'

Raavana's roaring beasts speeded their car.

Jatayu caught up again and sought reply,
'How once I too, like all my tribe, loved you.
But look at this acting hoodlum conduct.
Save yourself, Raavana, and pass me Sita.'

'Save yourself! Save yourself Jatayu. Flap away.'

Jatayu calmly, as ever, in a cut-glass loquacity,
'Raavana, remember the folly of the sand-piper
sleeping with uplifted feet so it keep the sky
from falling on its nest, on its young.
The wife of a king deserves protection.
What kind of king steals another man's wife?
Do the wise lay open their conduct for public censure?'

But Raavana cut in again that Jatayu should leave.
Still Jatayu persevered, 'Raavana, justice, for good or ill,
is grounded in a king. Let me help you
        recall your good deeds.'

Raavana felt irritated and flinched arrows at Jatayu.
                But the lord of sky-rovers
                began flapping his enormous wings.
                The flapping stirred up so much dust
                that a whipped storm
                beat the arrows back.

Jatayu then tried attacking the lions
                    so they would turn back

but snakes from dark creeps

        in the chariot stabbed outwards
        repelling the shocked old vulture.

Jatayu pleaded again and was ignored again.
Only then did he dare attack Raavana with beak and claws –
        he cut into Raavana.

Mortified, yet still Raavana would rather injure
than kill this valorous bird
        so he feebled Jatayu with a punch.

Jatayu flew back at Raavana
        but the latter finally saw red-mist!!!

With a Chandrahasa, his precious sword,
        two smotes tattered Jatayu's beautiful old wings.

It's said that every bird
        from as far here to the outer-midst

            for a spell fell silent

            when it was struck by Jatayu's soaring
pain note, by his crystal-cut pure cry-note

that suffered disintegration
    soon as the Chandrahasa

       gaped his throat.

Raavana's amphibian car streaked the airy pathways –
    he felt bad
witnessing the bravest all-time raja of birds
and friend to all in all kingdoms
    dumped between banyans as so much trash.

Book Fourth: You Hot Monkey!

~

Chapter One: Hole Block Bleeding Blunder

Sugreeva, a monkey, recalls two buffaloes and then his own brother, Bali.

~

'There was once a buffalo gang, their leader, Toraapa
   was a shocking white beast:
one day he must have lost his mind, ho . . .
Toraapa started horning to death all males in his tribe!

He was soon butchering the whole male gang
so he was the sole bull among his cow wives.

One Toraapa wife was pregnant and thinking:
      What if I bloating a boy, Mmwwohh!?
      Toraapa will horn him.

      She fled for a cave
and gave birth to a fulsome black buffalo she named Toraapi.

She fed Toraapi her milk
            soured with tales

about his father's death spree.

Toraapi hatched only hatred for his dad,
he daily sharpened his horns and at night
    he came down yonder
measuring his hooves against his father's hooves.

When Toraapi's hooves were big as Toraapa's hooves
he came down the mountain. And what did he do?
He first of all started gorging his sex appetite
    by bursting his pent bull-hood

                on his dad's wives!
Toraapi mated with each Toraapa cow

       even his own sweet mummy-ji!

Powering across the land, massed with his polluted wives,
the father, Toraapa, brimming in his whiteness
    called out monster-voiced,

"What bull dare soil my wives, Mmwwohh!?"

Leaking creams and red-eyed,
Toraapi burst his spunky voice, "It was I, yourrrrr
sson! These all are now become my wiiives!!!"

The father, hopping with rage, burst dry earth.
Then stamped his hooves and charged at the son
but the son wiggled aside: hornswoggler! Dainty boy.

Turning about, Toraapa charged at the boy again.
    Again, dainty boy.
        This tarupping charging
        back and hard and hard again
        till sundown ended
when the dad getting dizzied.

    Only then Toraapi fighting fair –
his rock-sharpened pike horns
        he horned into the dad guts!
    Toraapa was burst – flooding into his death.

    Toraapi then becomes big buffalo boss?
No-no, said the gods
sickened by Toraapi's toppling of the father.
They said he must fight his match, a monkey,
known as Bali, to prove his right to be a ruler.

So up stepped bad-black Toraapi
    to unsettle *our* monkey kingdom.
Bali was ready, "Oho buffalo!
Feel this right arm strength. This fist alone
will crumble your lungs, ho!" "I am Toraapi!

Mmmwwwohhhh!!!

Feel my hoof spur!

I burst a father who fought Sea and made it cry out
as spray.

Meet your Dead-God."

Bali, who was used to cracking off
mountain peaks and tossing them about like nits,
grappled with Toraapi.

Toraapi dainty: Bali brisk. One was flung up:
one flopped backwards. Reiterative deadlocking.

Bali addressed Toraapi,
"These fields are too loose for a full fight.
Come to a cave-yard where you see my gusto, ho!"
Toraapi must have feared that if Bali faced
defeat he may escape by flying across the trees
so he gladly followed through a hole
            to a cramped cave aside the ocean.

Bali told me, "Hang about by this hole, youngster,
so I can return this way once I've killed him, yo."

I kept my feet at the hole for many moons,
then one dawn
        streaming across the watery surface:

pale-red blood, the colour of monkey blood.

Bali must be dead, I thought. God bless Bali.
Our monkey advisers made me, as Bali's younger bro,
the king: King Sugreeva!

As Bali was dead, my army blocked the hole
with a mountain pushed over it to keep out Toraapi.

BUT, Bali was not dead, ho! He'd finally killed Toraapi
because Toraapi hadn't seen the cave-space
        was too small
        for him to charge.

Bali was all over the hulking buffalo
and killed him by cracking off a Toraapi horn
      then piercing him in the guts with it.

So why, you must be thinking, was Toraapi's
      blood pale-red as monkey blood?
At Toraapi's death, the gods had showered Bali
with flowers:
pollen and petals must have mixed-in with Toraapi's blood
to make it pale-red as it spread in the ocean.

           Bali tried returning up the hole
to be dancing his victory dance – hole blocked.
Bali must have thought that I blocked the hole
      to kill him, ho!
So Bali ripped Toraapi's mighty head off
and threw it so hard at the blocked hole
that the hole shattered into daylight. What a monkey.

Then seeing me on the throne as the new king
must have proved my cunning. Bali rushed at me
slapping me wildly. Not a word could I blurt.

"Entomb me? Coward bro!" he kept saying
as he kept slapping me. I only got free from the snappy
    slaps when I made it to Matanga.'

Chapter Two: The Love Pact

Rama meets Sugreeva.

~

Burgeoned brooding primordial buffoonish trees
husking their mushroomy
        honk about the free-drifting
vales and hills –
        the free-drifting vales and hills
                cooped with paranormal
                beings and goofy beasts.

Rama and Lakshmana trudged diligent there,
certain that Sita was taken by Soorpanaka and her ilk.

Rama remained shocked at his own shocked state
on returning to the cottage, after battle,
        and not finding Sita indoors.
He had madly dashed from ant to bird to deer to ravine
        crawling for news about Sita
and had stooped before banana, custard apple and bright
star clusters

then fallen before the chakravaka birds that sleep alone
           but they just sealed their eyes
               self-cuddling
                        on lotus beds.

Then he'd pleaded with Godavari river
      but of course Godavari kept schtum
fearing Raavana
      and watched instead Rama
hurling himself deep into feeble heart-breaking begging.

And now what chance landing upon his moiety,
his heart's half somewhere in this wilderness?
Walking foot-sore weeks and weakening
and scarce trained by Sage Viswamithra
for zooming upon a captured fellow . . .

Novices travelling hopelessly south
seeking support for recovering a noble lady.
Novices are in utter distress.
Help please, urgently for two
who have now fallen asleep beneath a tamarind tree.

As it happens, above, on a branch sat a monkey
who saw the brothers holding hands in their sleep
      united like the nail and the quick.
      Such brotherly affection
drew tears from the monkey for his own brotherly rift.

The tears hit Rama on the cheeks and woke him.

Rama lectured his brother against crying
and only stopped when he heard from overhead,

'It is me
        who is crying for loss of his brother's love.
I am an exiled king. I am requiring justice.

You do not seem to be sent by my brother, to kill me, ho.'

The brothers made acquaintance with Sugreeva.
Repasting with the exiled king and his army, they heard
Sugreeva's tale that ended thus,

'And here in Mount Matanga I idle about safely.
        Bali is cursed by Sage Matanga
that if he step into these precincts his skull
        will shatter most fragmentatiously!

In the meanwhile, my brother has reclaimed the throne
and also he is bagging for his rampant pleasure
        my wife, my Ruma.'

Rama was hooked by Sugreeva's grief,
'That scandalous abductor of your queen.
My own loss shows it's a looty-mark on my name.

I must become a brother to your cause, but how?'

                Sugreeva replied, 'Ho Rama,
                can you beat Bali?'

To test Rama they went where seven trees stood in a row.
Mountainous trees surviving four dissolutions of the universe.
Their branches swept so high they flopped into the heavens.
Measureless seemed the span from the base to the crown.

Said Sugreeva, 'Bali can shake this leafy tree leaving it
leafless, blank.'
Bali's body absorbs half the strength of the enemy he kills

      so his power is rare, ho!

These days, Bali's chest, when he is fighting, becomes thick
      as one of these trees?

          Can your arrows even pierce . . . ?'

Rama's response: focus. He twanged his bow
whose resonance echoed through hills and valleys.
Then Rama shot an arrow BUT not

through just one tree. Rama's arrow went through

    tree two   tree three

    tree four and so on till it shot through

all seven trees in a row

BUT not only that

it carried on through the seven ooperworlds

AND not only that

it carried on through the seven seas
and through all things in seven
before retiring to its nesting point in Rama's quiver!

All who had seen Rama's arrow-miracle bowed.

'Is more than my wildest surmise. I beg forgiveness.
You are truly the saviour who can be ridding Bali.
            A while ago we saw Raavana
            flying with a woman.'

Rama near swooned at how smirched he must appear
to have lost his wife. He became withdrawn awhile.
'Surely it must be your wife, hey.
Once we have removed Bali, I pledge
to summon a monkey army for your cause.'

Chapter Three: RAMA

Sugreeva and Bali fight for their right to the monkey throne.

~

● **Wahay Bali! You fight me!'**

Sugreeva's roar shot brazen over the mountains.
Bali bounced back a roar from his cave bed
as his eyes spat fire and he ground his teeth,

'Wahay, wahay, wait up, youngster!'

Bali's wife, the moonlike Tara, cautioning,
'Ho, he would not be putting a foot your way.
He may be inspirited by the power of this Rama human,
    talk is spreading about this invincible archer . . .'

'My cracking wife, your voice is nightingale
-ish
    and your style is peacockian
    but you ladies tell-tale bicker-snicker.

I hear Rama wears Truth's crown.
Could such a man, who sacrificed his right to the throne
upon a kid brother, could he meddle between brothers
by siding with one, with my sly brother, yo?'

'Sugreeva is still your blood, ho.
     Is he not younger?
Besides, who does not deserve a hearing?'
         Afraid to push the matter further,
         Tara stood back
as Bali seemingly expanded his frame in battle punch lust.

    From behind a rock,
    Rama saw this giant
    and whispered, 'Lak-
    shmana, is there any
    rival body-spectacular
    in the world?'

         Lakshmana now
         had misgivings,
         'Is Sugreeva trying
         to involve you
         in more than a
         common rift
         between monkeys?
         Of the brothers, who
         is correct here?'

'Do you not think
brotherly strife
can be pinned
on all species?'

      'We are keshatriya
      who stand in the op
      -en . . .'

Silence. The monkeys slapped their broadened chests
and grappled.

      The balls of their feet clashed,
emitted sparks, sparks gobbed from their eyes
but Bali was soon smashing up his wee brother.

Smashing him up till
      Rama drew an arrow

then out from behind his hiding place he shot it hard.

Like a needle passing though ripe papaya
      the arrow sped thoroughly through Bali's back.

Bali was struck,

'Who, moulded by earth bend me wriggling dying?
Who cowardly nail my meat, so hard, hey?'

Bali was now spilling blood from his prodigious heart.

Dying to perceive his killer
with one inordinate shakti
he roared his fingers back into his own torn juicy depths
    with all his might

            he screamed

yanking out through his own front – the arrow!

Dead-God, Yama, gawped at Bali with crazy awe.
Gods generally applauded brave Bali.

Bali almost fainting, read the name on the arrow

R   A   M   A

and double-checked the name in shock
and again.

RAMA

The shock of defeat and death was nothing to Bali
    against the spiritual shock
that this demon-foe was become his foe.

To himself: so my wife, my Tara, was right . . .
How could I be so uppity, hey . . . ?

Rousing his final terms, Bali said,
'O Rama, lord of
culture, justice and conduct –
     have you kicked into dust your own codes?
Who'll now wear Virtue's badge? You chuck it lightly
by slaughtering the head of a monkey clan.
     I was revering you, hey.'

Rama, who had come out from behind his rock,
'In your hot-blood you have shown little respect
for your brother's virtues. He protected the throne
     but you slapped him about for it.'

'What is this judgement, hey? When two parties
are in dispute how can you befriend one
     and back-stab the counter-party?'

Said Rama, 'Sugreeva sought your mercy
instead you gave grief to a meek brother —' 'You won,'
said Bali, interrupting, 'Sugreeva's support
     against Raavana?
Is like courting a rabbit to tame a lion . . .

     One pleading word here
and I would have died
rucking to arrange on a platter this Raavana;
     returning, safe
for your misfiring eyes, Sita.' Lakshmana
stepped in, 'Do not blame Rama. We promised
Sugreeva we'd keep back

185

whilst you brothers fought. You been brass neck:
you stole a kid brother's wife, your sister-in-law!'

The sails of the wind were lifting
and eager to sail Bali away, but Bali puffed hard and,

> 'Heyhey! Rama and Lakshmana,
> is blind judgement! In our monkey
> world is apt to take a brother's
> wife. Becomes my duty
> to protect Ruma once
> my brother scram. My kid
> brother betrayed my trust.
> Plotting against me and leaping
> to the throne ahead of
> my son, Angada. And took my
> Tara to bed. You talking
> incest . . . treachery?'

Said Rama, 'Under my brother, Bharat's reign in Ayodhya,
we are here to assist his rule by establishing peace
    wherever we please.'

> 'Human marital customs
> are alien to us. What is
> wedlock to us, hey? Our
> monkey laws and ways
> are not human customs
> of those who come from
> far-off, from Ayodhya.'

Said Rama, 'I am aware of your monkey ways.
You own plenty insight to know right from wrong
but when you rule barbarously
it befalls on man to hunt wild animals.
Remember man is granted power
        to trap in pits and with nets
          whatever beast is a bane.'

                'Is an eye-opener

    when my eyes are

closing.

    A hunter kills me

                if I'm edible or a

    threat. Was I either,

hey? Lord Rama,

                you are bent on
          good deeds – I must take

    death by your spear

as God's own judgement.'

 Bali's last words,

'Hey Angada . . .

my son . . .

make quick shift to the new . . .

seek peace with your un—'

In Bali's dying, Rama said, 'Fear not, great Bali.
Your son and your wife

are under my protection now.'

Rama handed back Ruma, to her husband, Sugreeva.
Rama watched them smiling,

watched them *yo!* and behold
whilst he shuffled off. But then he caught Tara's stare,

'Now you have trapped him hey, will you eat him?
Where is the good in parting two so in heaven with love.

O noble, noble man!'

Chapter Four: Monsoon Causing up to No Good

Rama grieves for Sita.

~

No animal stirred for the period. Period.
The sky rumbled and a golden lash
cut the sky for lightning. The earth on a wizened wind
sough song, was alliteratively bumbling big drops
    from Indra's kohl clouds,
was metaphorically raining constant cats and dogs!

In the room where he and Sita had slept, he became downcast.
He was stormed by pangs that uncertainty itself
and uncertainty of an outcome were drowning him in.

Mountain water rushing down with flesh and fowl
served to bring on greater guilt about his wife
and how she, from him, lay washed away . . .

Real or hallucinatory, between trees
peahens walking with their mates tormented him.
He who lived daily without eating. So lost in his thoughts

he did not even brush away a termite mound
growing about him.

Flaws coalesced in a mind abuzz as ever with his wife . . .
     He chased his mind after a girl
in flowing silks for armour, with a bow of sugarcane
and flowers for arrows – how could she have felled him so
softly?
     He could not handle the irony.

And fell upon the gravest point mankind attains
and couldn't haul up his head from the mire.
Lakshmana saw it all and felt sad
and could have said: obey a father and lose a wife . . .

Instead Lakshmana interceded to groom his brother
for the formal mood, 'Rama, as you once told me:
     passion breeds mental chaos.
This desire, this passion – how far from duty
you are sinking. Rain that begets our earthly food –
must we not open our arms to it
and take on the storm or if we are sunk under . . . Let
the rain feed you with its own sweet harmony
so you shed worldly grief
so you become fortified for our spiritual observance.
How else win back Sita-jee?
Come, let us turn to our allies for support.'

'O brother, Sita and I are but one heart.
If you tear us apart, what are we but bleeding for the rest . . . ?'

What could Lakshmana reply but look outside.

Outside, season over, nature's traffic
        cheeped and jippered
with swans, cranes and other aquatic birds in aerial concourse,
new fish flexing about in the streams
and areca palms ripened their fruits in golden bunches
around flowers
whilst crocodiles spanned out in the sun.
Peacocks furled their tails and gave up their love games.

And Rama holding a white thumba flower
slowly managed his grief
whilst huffy Lakshmana marched to Kiskinda.

Lakshmana would find a baggy-eyed Sugreeva,
baggy clearly from too much partying with molasses wine,
with honey wine. Or so the sweet air implied.

Tara was sent at the palace gates
to receive and then with her fine words placate Lakshmana.
Sugreeva's conscience was easily pricked about a mission
with the mega post-monsoon army he'd promised.

Chapter Five: Not so by Thiruvengadam

Sugreeva informs Hanuman about where he should search for Sita.

~

Sugreeva became himself and readied an army to locate Sita,
but first things first, where the heck is the enemy?
A search party was led by a nigh-on midget monkey,
Hanuman,
for only Hanuman could come up trumps.
Hanuman, that startling white-bodied, white-haired monkey
quietly memorised all the details Sugreeva imparted.

'Hey Hanuman, you are my most trusted.
Report to me within thirty days where exactly Sita is captive.
Now absorb my words.
Head mostly southwards
      but comb the land from west to east and down.

Go past the cloud-topping Vindhya mountain peaks
and search for Sita in every nook of the mountain ranges
then after that range check along the lovely rivers

of Bhagirathi, Sarayu and Kausiki
perhaps even afield to the Yamuna river
        and the mountains in which it rises.

Then to the Sarasvati, the Sindhu and the Sona
        with their jewel-sparkling waters,
and nearby is Mahi and then nearby is Kalamahi
with its hilly and wooded banks.

        Still no Sita?

Sweep across to Magadha's great villages,
        search in the kingdoms of Brahma-mala, Malava,
in Pundra and Anga; look where the silk worm is bred
        and where silver is mined.

Then you will reach the range called Hemakuta
on whose gold-topped towers divine damsels descend
to spend their hours composing and singing lyrics
which lull even birds and beasts to sleep.

Listen hard, Hanuman. Do not let any holy spot
wobble your legs from the main task.
If you find yourself by that holiest mountain,
        Thiruvengadam:
I say, stiffen up. Back off.

        A visit to this spot is your instant
heaven but seek all reward after Sita is found.
Besides, how likely is Raavana

to be rooted at this sacred ladder?

Your time is limited. Tarry not, yo.
Look next in the hills, perhaps the hills of Mandara
where there are people with ears that are
                            curtains draping
                            down their body:
ears so long they lollop below their lips,
and peoples whose faces are made from iron
and hopping peoples who schlep about on a single leg.
All these peoples or what they are
                    eat only mammal flesh.

Next look where the beautiful gold-skin hunters
who are known as human tigers live –
they live underwater in hill and forest homes.

Still no Sita? Then veer for the island of Yava-dvipa
        which can only be reached
        by crossing over hills and seas,
and only you, my magnificent Hanuman, can make this trek.
Inside the mountains are many lions, tigers, elephants
        and boars roaring the long sundial day
enchanted only by the echo of the din of their own sounds.

Yava-dvipa has seven kingdoms
where is mined gold and silver.
Look carefully among these terrifying islands
for here are enormous arsooras
        that catch creatures by their shadows.

Then by nibbling on the shadow they nibble
>
> throu
> gh the
> creature's actual flesh!

Thereby is a mountain where is the greatest dancer.
Whilst she dances your ears will fill with erotic song.
Hema is her name. Hema will help you in,
> but if you enter her mountain
> you enter Death, yo,
for you cannot give her grooves the slip.
Your ears will be like bees gumped in the music's honey.
And you will drop dead when her song drops off.

Do not nowhere near enter the shadow of Hema's mountain
> for the shadow goes against the sun
> for that shadow is Hema's crafted handiwork.

Then you will come upon a sea clad with serpents
where you will greet the blood-red waters
that are said to be redder even than the waters of Lohita
> where live fierce Mandehas
> who are huge as boulders
and who hang upside down from mountain peaks.
> They are daily burnt by the sun
> and they daily slip into the ocean
> and then return to hang upside down
> again, each day.

Soon you are at the ocean of pure water
where is said all will be floating at Time's end.
Go on all fours or fly fast through this scape
    for the sound here will be unbearable –
wailing creatures of the deep are heard
for they cannot bear to look at
    the horse-faced son of Wrath-God
who is held trapped here. Who knows why all this happens?

Once out of the ocean you are at Jatarupa,
    a mountain where lives a serpent
with a thousand heads nested atop its head.
Keep watching him for he is still: silent.
Yet when he moves he's reared at you
    before you knew he was there.

Past Jatarupa, there is a crevice clefting the earth –
peep down and you may glimpse the serpent Sesha
who is white like the moon. He upholds Earth on his coils.
    Nobody can travel any further.

Beyond is the region where several gods roam –
no sun or moon is here but darkness only for mortal eyes.
    This is as far as monkeys tread
    for we do not know what is beyond
    except is pure walkabout.'

Storing in his capacious monkey mind every detail,
diminutive Hanuman was ready for his biggest challenge.

Rama added, 'You know not Sita but
you can observe her by her toe-nails
glowing red as rubies. Or observe her heels
for learned men have compared them to a quiver . . .'
Lost in sighs, Rama ceased his description.

Chapter Six: In Bird Brain

Hanuman seeks help in locating Sita.

~

For thirty days Hanuman's army
    scoured mountains and valleys,
passed impassable torrents and climbed
unclimbable crags, ran alongside temples with hidden
side-doors leading to heaven
        and still Raavana and Sita

    where are they?

Hanuman called despairing from a mountain tableland,
'Great Jatayu, if you had not died
only your vision could have enlightened us now.'
At this, what seemed a vile looking raksassy
hobbled towards him with giant wings
all skin-marred, with guzzy feathers.
It spoke in a cut-glass voice,

'I am the vulture Sampathi, Jatayu's elder brother.

Long ago, we were parted
and now I hear him mentioned as being dead.
Who killed him? Who would kill my gentle brother?'

Hanuman explained how they had found Jatayu
dangling from trees and had buried him
offering several fat deer in sacrifice
to the spirit of the departed so Jatayu could find peace.

Relieved Sampathi explained how the brothers had been
parted,
'. . . we would skim and float in the higher skies. One day
we flew higher than ever so we the heavens might glimpse.
We flew higher and crossed the path of Sun-God
who became vexed. Perhaps he assumed we were being
impudent.
He bore his full heat on us. I said to Jatayu,
fly away! I shielded him under my wings whilst he escaped.

My feathers, as you see are burnt. I tried flying away
but my propulsion flapped me to this peak.
I have been here unheard the while, gripping to dear life,
for my inner vision says redemption from the gods will come
when I hear *Rama* uttered within my earshot.'

At this, Hanuman and his army cried in one voice,

Rama Zindabad!

Sampathi's feathers healed and as he rose

his wings were again
soft broad arches cruising through the effortless skies!

The feathery monarch heard about Hanuman's mission
and recalled from aloft, 'If it is Raavana you seek,
you have come too far east. He was carrying a woman back to
Lanka
and that is direct south.
My brain has divine powers and has sensed only this:
Raavana holding Sita captive in the Asoka gardens.

Now I must take my leave, I must return
to lead my tribe since there is no Jatayu.'

Chapter Seven.one: Jawman

The army considers how to reach Lanka.

~

All you who would mock a fellow humanoid
by jesting how they're a monkey,
I say it's neither a fun-mock nor a wise-jest.
Now watch me show you how cussing a fellow
    by calling them *monkey*
      is dread ironic!
Listen to the true tale about wee Hanuman

whose army despaired at the great ocean between them
and Lanka. No flying monkey could make the perishing
journey.
Jambavan, the wise bear, whose army had recently
hooked up with Hanuman, spoke thus,

'Youthful when I was, I leapt 200 yojanas high
    and circumambulated
about Vishnu's triple-stride through the universe.

Ancient as I am now, I can still leap up to 100 yojanas
but my upper-leap is shot with age.
One is here who can leap greater than I could ever.'

Angada stepped in, 'It falls to none other
but I must attempt this leap.'
                  Jambavan bowed before the warrior,
saying,
     'Kings or a king-to-be, such as you are,
send servants whose honour is served best
by attending upon the duty. You are the darling and the boast,
we serve to defend our hope that is enshrined in you
and your king, King Sugreeva.

Look not around Hanuman. Who is the one
who alone can make the leap and live?

                You only
can reach Lanka, Hanuman. So wealthy in wisdom and might,
yet Hanuman, why do you tarry?'

But Hanuman looked back
like one who is wading through the cloths of night
and to himself
has become a benighted cloth he cannot unfold from.

'Hanuman, to your own self it seems
you are lost . . .
                Hanuman, who you truly are
                I will find him for you now.

Hanuman, your backbone is made from a jewelled club,
your body moulded from a trident. Hanuman, your head
was chiselled from a diamond discus. Hanuman, your father
is Wind-God
and he placed that club, that diamond and that discus
in your mother's mouth. Greatly against her will.
Thirty swarthy months past
and Hanuman, against natural curving-time
you coalesced into a baby
issuing from your mother's
mouth.

Child when you were
                you could leap up high.
Red like a twilight was something shimmering in the west
and you thought it must be a rare fruit: one day,
        you leapt to pluck it.
Hanuman you leapt
        over 300 yojanas
                and you headed for the sun!

                Not so impressed was Indra.
He smacked you with a thunderbolt
and to a mountain peak
you fell.
Your jaw was broken. Even your name
comes from this event, Hanu means jaw. You are Jawman.

Brahma felt bad for you – your bite was weak.
Brahma compensated you by making you invincible in battle.

Brahma gave you freedom from the jaws of Death,
though Death – only you can choose when you seek him.
Hanuman, only you so tired of life
      will choose the way you die.
Hanuman, only you if you tire of life
      will choose when you die.

So threatened by your new powers was your father,
that as your father he was able to lay a curse on you.
He cursed you so your own powers you would never know.
      That curse, I have powers to repeal.
You are the son and heir of Wind-God
and earning his power and glory is your birth right.'

Hanuman's heart surged at the bulletin.
Whilst Jambavan performed the service
Hanuman swung his tail and with each bow-shape of his tail
the army watched Hanuman making his mark in the world!

Jambavan calling the while,
'Arise Hanuman and keep arising. You are our saviour!
Hanuman, you are taller than any monkey.
Hanuman, but you can rise to any stature.
You can grow so big, Hanuman,
      bigger even than Vishnu
      when he strode through the stars
      dunking down into hell
         the demon Mahabali . . .'

Hardly was Jambavan being heard

for Hanuman's head, Hanuman's stonking simian bonce
    was bigger than each bosomy cloud

each Hanuman caress-breath

                causing a floccus

a gasping of *hie!hie!*
        that drizzled

each cloud into Hanumanian creams . . .

The army bowed to their massive darn hard leader
who was already beating against the heat
hot-trotting his monkey power through the murky ocean!

Chapter Seven.two: The Sex Threat

Hanuman inspects Lanka and searches for Sita.

~

Now watch this for astute monkey machinations.
Hanuman in Lanka, fly-size, exploring the capital.
He recorded information about the golden gateways
and dazzling dark buildings that seemed, at their height
                    hovering in air.
He noted how Lanka was divided into four complex quarters
by wide roads and multi-storied mansions.
Each quarter was heavily guarded by raksassy armies
geared for a gory good ruck.

He watched raksassy going about their business
wearing varied looks and all seemed to, snug-like, fit in,
from the full-bodied beauteous type to the odd ilk.

The odd ilk walked around bazaars and along rivers,
some were dwarfish and held hands with a monster-
shadow sized fellow that had a single
eye or ear,

some were lying in the open with piping necks
and were snogging those with knots and braids
for dark and wan skin,
some with every bodily pore
hair-crammed were being tickled by a lover with a jackal's
jaw and nose,
some with faces of boars were dancing
with some who had faces of buffalo,
some with goat or dog head
sang to their lover who had lions' lips and horses' brows,
some with feet of cows were carrying
the lover who had feet of mules
and all lay or walked or danced or sang freely
under the Lord's happy sun . . .

Hanuman flew away from the bright light
and approached Raavana's palace with its prodigious
palace moat.
The moat-waters were whipped by a local wind
so they circled with a sea power, all the while
inhabited by sharks and serpents.

Flying over the moat, as serpents lunged up
to gulp a monkey snack, Hanuman went indoors
into Raavana's palace
which resembled Indra's Amaravati.

The palace alone was 100 yojanas long and as wide,
a bamboozling city in itself with winding staircases

leading underground to endless chambers
and further down bunkers
and from ground-level rising up to the heavens
each floor was a web of narrow walkways and rooms
and intricate hidden chambers and trapdoors.

Hanuman went down one convolution
and spied Raavana's ditched brides
all downcast along winding staircases
and in narrow anterooms and further down in bunkers.
The ditched brides were being fanned by fit young attendants
ready for the gigolo action
save that the wives still sought the top dog!

Hanuman flew through a hall
and all about so many raksassy ladies sleeping
on the patterned rugs and flashing their sand-dune buttocks:
some semi but most, most definitely, unclad
save for the odd cat's-eye gem about the neck.
Many wore pearl necklaces that were like white water-birds
rising and falling between their breasts. Lascivious
carnival met Hanuman
who watched ladies sleeping atop each other's breast
or caught in a thigh; so many unmarried ladies
surrendered to Raavana's hard party calamity!

Hanuman was ever the thinker when it was most required.
And here he was thinking
how it is the mind which makes the senses perform
good or bad deeds.

The digressive mind become dissolute
        must become subject to flesh:
whilst the flesh hoots and toots the mind is left wafting itself.

Yet I feel my mind, he wondered, must be well-ordered
enough
for as I look at beauty, unparallel'd willy-nillying
naked, up-for-nooky, on the floor, I can master my lust;
my mind feels bound to duty and thus to purity;
it can observe these ladies
        without treacherous quickie lust.

Thus he flew into Raavana's bedroom
fearing to sight the cynosure of beauty, Sita.

He saw a statue of Lakshmi and there beneath
        banking the room
the lord, in his incomparably magnificent crystal bed, asleep.

Hanuman flying close to admire
    battle scars from centuries past:
    great famed wounds
    from Airavata's tusks and Vishnu's discus
and his shoulders
    scored with Indra's thunderbolts.

Hanuman gawped at the arms rounded as iron clubs,
the fingers perfectly chiselled and enamelled
so each twenty hands looked a five-hooded snake.

Hanuman remembered his own mission to locate Sita
so it's paramount to avoid being detected,
he thought about how ambassadors
who fail to keep to the article of orders –
surely they betray their master's cause.

Just then Raavana began to steam
and rolled around in his silken sheets.
The beauteous rough-haired lady at his side,
could it be Sita? The lady woke up the lord
who was tossing and turning in his sleep.

Hanuman was a speck atop a chandelier, hearing,
'You know Lord, you have my permission
to end this pained tossing I see you stewing yourself each night

    in.'

'Ah, Mandodari, my dear wife, what is it you mean?'
'Take Sita against her will. Why seek her permission?'

    Raavana leapt from bed,
    'I must be at her now.'

Chapter Seven.three: The Death Threat

Raavana meets Sita during the night.

~

The lord's sea heaving,
   the lord alighting from his crystal chariot.

His torch bearers had woken Sita but she had refused
the seat in her pavilion.

His attendants set before her stunning jewels.
From the moon's horribly lit-up response
she knew they were rare godly things
        but did not look upon them.

Hanuman was floating, above a Simsapa tree,
            on a moonbeam
for he had at last sighted Sita. He wondered to himself,
how if Rama should dry the ocean
and starve earth
for such a prize as Sita it may be worth the while . . .

The lord's grottos, orchards and pleasure gardens
seemed washed in indigo.

      The lord appreciated scale,
small-scale Lanka
where he wuthered
in heavenly made
summers
and now at night
whilst constellations held overhead
he relaxed in the evening breath,
relaxed in Sita's breath . . .

He was all concentration.
His dazzling copper eyes watched her.
His teeth, white as the moon, glinted.
He appeared to be soaking up

Sita's heartbeat.

He was crepuscular: between desire and despair.
Only the wings of his nostrils

                  elevating

basking

inhaling the essence of woman, pure woman . . .

'Brahma, my grandfather, never created beauty

as you are beauty. I have flown upon his finest works.
    Not even Ahalya . . .
Your earthly coloured golds and browns are a perfection,
near an offence to aspect.

Even your bare feet, their tan ripening skin alone
   blinds me, beheads me.

But how sad it becomes you sitting on this green verge,
   in bark-skin.'

Said Sita, 'I am where I am brought down to.'

'Is it your custom to dress your hair in a single braid,
   to begin new love
     by remembering, by mourning?'

Sita closing her ears at such implicating talk.

Raavana continuing, 'I too am plunged
   in a furrow of memory,
my brain grooved with your imprint . . .
   You are my grief, my solace.
   We are our grief, our solace.

You have seen, all the ladies who adore me
fell at my feet of their own accord.
I need not ever be flirting or stoop.

Ah, dark eyes Lady, have I not been courteous?'

Sita, head downward the while, finally lifted
    a blade of grass
and laid the blade of grass wall-like

    between herself and Raavana,

'Do you think reputation enough to win me?
Do you not know I am the wife of Lord Rama?'

'I would not ever touch you against your desire.'

    'I am as good as touched.
Yet I will never be touched except by my Lord.'

'Have you, in essence, not touched me, Sita,
    when you chose to
break free from your Circle of Chastity?'

'How brave you are! Breaking a woman
    by crafting her off
behind her husband's back.'

'My only craft my cup of beggary
hungering only for the touch of your alms.'

Raavana's lust abating and rising with each
soaring wondrous note around Sita's cool breath.
'Where is your Lord of the Deerskin this past ten months?
    He has shed you into my circle.'

Sita gave mockery for mockery,
'So many wives, chuker, circle you it seems.
Why not come round to your wives? Do not give me
these jewels. Give them straight
to your wives. Why wake up the night
  begging before another man's
  to-the-death beloved?'

Raavana sighed. Then ordered Sita's attendants,
'As before, give my queen any luxury she desire.
Bounty my queen with a perfect mango each day.
All pleasures are my queen's suitors.'

When Raavana and his attendants departed,
Sita stayed on the verge. Fearlessly alone.

Hanuman watched Sita starting to cry.

Her arms embraced her legs. She sang to herself.

  'If Rama is my heart
  where is my heart beating beating?
  If Rama is my soul
  where is my soul beating beating beating?
  You are my light you will never go out . . .'

Then rushing for a branch
  over which to hurl
  her long single plait
  as a noose

and up there
herself to be hanging!

Chapter Seven.four: You Shot-Hot Monkey!

After meeting Sita Hanuman becomes angered.

~

' . . . no, please, dear Lady, I come from Rama.
I am here to help you. Rama is thinking about you always.
I can try and fly you back to Rama. I can save you,'
said Hanuman as he grew to his new normal size.
He put on Sita's Kosala dialect
rather than speak in his regional tongue.

Sita threw herself on the floor,
crying even more now at being stopped by a . . . raksassy?
She questioned the monkey about Rama, at length.
And was impressed by his proper sequencing of thought.

She calmed and even seemed pleased
when Hanuman gave her Rama's wedding ring
        with RAMA inscribed upon it.
She sighed, 'The more I touch this ring
        the more I am hearing Rama.'

In exchange, so Rama knew Hanuman had met Sita,
    memento to memento,
Sita took from her hair a pearl that rested on a gold leaf,
    her Choodamani.

'This pearl was plucked from the Great Milk Ocean
by the god Indra. He honoured my father with it.
O Hanuman, tell Rama I always think only of him.

    Tell him Raavana has not laid on me
    a breath or touch.

Even as you say, Hanuman, you could try to rescue me now,
and I bless you for it.

    In our customs
    no one else must rescue me.
    Only Rama himself, with or without his army,
    must rescue me.'

'Rama will be inspired to know how firm you remain.
We will be here within weeks.'

Sita left for her chambers.

Hanuman felt so bad for Sita's plight
that he lost himself.

Becoming again massive. So massive that he

trudged
rampant over

Asoka Vana

**pulling up trees
with his mega-
bare grip
then dunking
them back deep
in the ground
upside down**

**till the tree
roots were
all freaked
in the wind
whilst lolling**

at the

moon.

The pleasure garden was a horror show.

Raavana got wind of the mess
and sent his army to capture the white monkey.

Raavana's bruisers saw a gross simian
stood by a hall, cross-armed and whistling
whilst admiring the black smoke he'd roused.

Hanuman lifted a shining golden pillar,
from the hall he'd crushed, then attacked the bruisers.
He killed a flank of raksassy
     before Jambumali arrived on the scene.

Jambumali was one of Raavana's friskiest bruisers,
with great tusks pronging from his gob,
with his trademark
     blazing white shirt and ear-rings
he stood atop a gate and assaulted arrows at Hanuman.

A half-moon tipped arrow slaked a monkey cheek.
Hanuman's face glowed like a full-blown autumn lotus.
Hanuman broiled with rage: a boulder at his feet,
he lifted it and chucked it with great hurl at Jambumali!

But Jambumali's thunderous arrows were a stymie.

Hanuman was rage-hard! Hanuman
smashed his wild body, like a rock, towards Jambumali
and as Jambumali fell down
Hanuman roared his fists into that pronged beastie.

Jambumali was overwhelmed like never before
and felt a few body-crushing blows queasy his guts.
     Then Hanuman smashed the tusks

back into Jambumali's cheeks!

He knocked Jambumali out for the count
    so bad
it became hard to distinguish Jambumali
from his shirt, his bow and arrows, his chariot and horses.
All was one vile heap thanks to one hot monkey!

    Hold on though.

    Raavana's son, Indrajit,
who'd been praying when he heard the monkey mayhem,
with his lethal powers he summoned a mantra
that can be applied just the once on a fellow.

    The mantra shot forth Shiva's net.

Hanuman fell to the ground tied by a net of sunlight.

    Unable to move.

And trapped in a hot-net for good.

Before Indrajit could reach Hanuman, from the distance
he saw the army rush forward and chain up Hanuman.
The soldiers hadn't worked out why the monkey was
    arms down-his-side and writhing in light.

The chains came on: Indrajit's net came off.

Indrajit bit his lip, for Shiva's noose cannot hold
    if any other bond has been laid over it.
Boundless ignorance takes charge, thought Indrajit
as he returned back to his nook and resumed his meditation.

Hanuman was scuffled away by the glory seekers.

When Raavana saw the giant white creature,
he was appalled, 'This is no mere monkey.
He must be a new creature
    made by the gods to tax me.'

Hanuman, who was bound and held, said,
'Yo, Raavana, I am here to tell you
Rama is invincible. Change or be changed up.'
Said Raavana, 'So you support Rama.
But how did you get to Lanka?'

    'I walked.'

When laughter in the hall ceased,
'The reward for your long walk is a short walk
 to death!'

'If I must die, one favour only I ask,
that you pick my death from two ways.'
Raavana, perked by this queer fellow, waved a hand
so Hanuman be heard.

'If I die the way of the monkey mother –

lock me in a store-room
with tastiest dishes and I will choke to death.

If I die the way of the monkey father –
wrap my tail in cloth
pouring oil on it then setting it alight.'

To placate the hall roars of *kill him!*
Vibishana said, 'Remember, the one murdering an envoy
violates the ancient law and descends
to that hell of heated jars, Taptakumbha.'

Raavana agreed and said, 'Let him be shamed;
a bezti that befits his punishment, his guilt.'
Vibishana muttering, 'I hear monkeys regard
the tail as precious. Let us serve him with his father's fate.'

Hanuman was dragged away to the Gentle Room.
His tail was dunked in oil and set alight.
Raksassy blew conches and trumpets made monkey-mocking
        ooh-oooh-ooohs at Hanuman's tail.

Except those of you who are monkey fun-makers
you must desist now your oooh-ooohing too
for that monkey, with swiftness wits, to escape his shackles
        shrank! Shrank! Once out of his
traps he began
enlarging and as he began carefully over-enlarging the flame
about his tail too was large
so that when that monkey was big as a building

227

the flame at the end of his hairy serpent tail was a fireball!

Then that mere monkey went ooh-oooh-ooohing as he leapt
from rooftop to rooftop with the wind
helping him swing and slap his flaming tail
    wherever he ooh-oooh-oooh'd!

Hanuman swung his thing all over the capital
before shrinking in size to flee.
In his wake: mansions, ramparts, gateways, watch-towers
loosened

                    and leaked
                their ores, coral,
              pearls and silver . . .

So to end present proceedings,
all you who would mock a fellow humanoid
by jesting how they're a monkey,
I say it's neither a fun-mock nor a wise-jest.
I hope it has been shown how insulting a fellow
    by calling them a monkey is dread ironic!
Now call a mate a monkey
and see how proud he feels when on his mind is
    hero-Hanuman
who by magic had not a hair singed on his tail!
               You monkey.

Chapter Eight: Emergency Raksassy Jaw Jaw

Raavana with his war cabinet.

~

Demons have all the backhander shortcuts
for getting a job done in double-time.
So Raavana had coolest denizens built
with fullest dodgy means in next-no-time.

Raavana was in no mood to enjoy his revamped palace,
stating to his advisers, 'This monkey has shot off
      having shot down our capital.'

Spoke, mighty commander-in-chief, Prahasta,
who'd led Raavana's armies against Kubera and the Devas,
'Rama has been bold sending a monkey in disguise.
Would it not become us if we changed into mortals
meddling in Rama's army to kill freely from within?
Otherwise what began with a monkey may not end
with a monkey. Next, challenging our rule
might be a flood of pesky mosquitos!'

He was cut short by the goofy giant, Mahodara,
a lumpen giant amongst giants,
'Let me get this monkey and all his allies.
I'll fee-fie-foe and drink their blood!
I'll piss it red in the lakes and wells
        from where sages sup water!'

Iron-club wielding, Vajradamshtra was straight in
spilling his unequivocally comic beans, 'Daaaat faaat
monkey has prepared us
dat fooood is making its own way for our mouuuuths.
It will be good fill for my club. Looook at my club!

Looook at its dribbling blood and flesh-lumps.
My club is 'ungry-'ungry! Listen, my club is saying,

Dis Rama, dis Hanuman is the gooooiest
        smell I ever been tell about.
                My iron tummy is 'ungry-'ungry!'

The advice was getting samey. Vibishana stood
till the cheers were snapped shut and all were seated,
'Great brother,
do not allow yourself to enter this manner.
You are everything to me, to us all:
        a father, a leader, a guru.

What grieves is that you may lose your throne
after all your austerities to gain great boons.
In a sense it was not a monkey tail

that hurt our great city
but the rightness flame raging inside Sita.
Let us cleanse ourselves of this sin.'

Silence.

Vibishana spoke softly, 'Anyone ever conquer the gods
and live victorious . . . long? Retribution
shadows each affronting action. My lord, I do not think
    you sought protection from mankind
    so why be rousing them to stand behind a flag?
What mighty force is commanding or commanded by such a
one
as Rama if his bow alone is sleep to armies? How simply
these two brothers scattered to the fourteen worlds
    Trishira and the mighty Kora.

Dear brother,
you may also remember Nandi's curse
after you mightily heaved the Kailas mountain . . . that
your end would be aided by monkeys . . . ?'

Vile silence.

Indrajit's eyes were yellow with venom,
'Winter clouds are big with thunder
    but do they bring
fresh rain? So it is false relations seek our favour
    but secretly, I think they seek change . . .
Protection? Were anyone so blind

                    seeking such a hand
as my foot-strong father who is holding our island
bound? This Rama dropped his throne
losing it to a kid brother. Would this befall my father?'

Vibishana persevered with his brother, 'O brother,
I beg you give up this wrangle with the gods.
Let us be dwelling in our sun and delighting in our fruits.
Should not a king be seeking alliance with his equals?
An army should never be undervalued
especially one devoted to a bloodthirsty cause. Do we have
cause in kind? Why keep a lovesick wife? Return
the damaged goods and win victorious peace, brother!'

Finally, Raavana rose, 'Remember
before Rama was born, I seized three worlds.
I have grown stronger: whatever Vishnu have I have more.
          So what power in Rama?

          You grieve me, Vibishana.
          Leave Lanka. I give you leave.
Look all about you and go, there I grant you freedom.

I say to you all, who could tolerate this,
what this saint Rama is, if he, not even touch,
          but cut our sister!
Do we even touch his wife? Did he not freely murder
          Mareecha, Trishira and the galloping Kora!

Is this the work of a saint-scholar or a butcher?

Even if we were to return Sita, we would capture Rama
      and offer the bride as freedom's price.
But why be returning Sita? I brought her freely
from my own forest where she has been tenanted.

      If she is comforted by our haunts
let her be haunted by our comforts.
         I declare she is my own property.

So be readying for some major bishboshing.
Let the lowerworlds and the ooperworlds come too!

Did we not kick out Kubera and take Lanka?
Did not Maya, so cower'd by me, give me his daughter,
my dear Mandodari, in marriage? How many cities
in the underworld have we not attacked and taken?

How did I unseat each foe –
      by taking the tusks of his elephant,
tusks never shattered under great thunderbolts,
that under the force of my jolts cracked like radishes.

How many gods? Did I not shake Shiva's hills
         like a rag
and loosen them from goblins and imps you all feasted
full year on?

I say, bring on man and bear and monkey and bird
and we shall thunder them past the chasms
      swirling about the cold universe!

Our pleasure grounds are verged on eternal victory!'

Raavana continued his riotous speech
till his fighters were whipped into wanton fury
and each atom of their being sparked for annihilation.

Chapter Nine: Madu Madya Honey-pot Hairdown Day!

The monkeys and bears celebrate their success.

∽

O golly golly gosh what a lot of dirty hooting
drunkard monkeys bonking any lot of lady
fellows in the randy vineyard with all for swinging
fulsome column donging orgy virility no-end
    and every josser monkey
    got some jiggy game
    till arm-linked hill-top
    bawdy song-along!

Hanuman forgetting himself on his way
to see his king and instead before the big
battle and for one last final fling leading Angada
and the gang not forgetting wise bear Jambavan
    and his crew
    to Maduvana
    to Daddymuck's
    vineyard.

There they rifled through the treasured store
and got a bit madu, or sozzled, on honey-wine madya,
drowning potfuls and banging for the female
honeypot! The female monkeys and bears
guarding the vineyard for bread-head boring
Daddymuck couldn't believe their saucy fortune!!!

>Their uber-cock-
>a-hoopery when
>they'd put down
>their weapons
>and taken up
>an entirely
>lustier sort
>of weapon.

O golly golly cheeeeeky gosh!

Monkeys and bears bumbling down the hills
and chucking pot or vat in the air and crocking
across the grove. More bosky freedom! More madu!
More tupping! Till Daddymuck roared ***Enufff!***

Enough? Not quite enough just yet, sahib!
They thumped the partypooper who galloped off
to find King Sugreeva. The king settled the debt.

>Daddymuck
>stroked his
>white beard
>with gold-bag
>gleeeeeee!!!

Rama and Sugreeva were sure good news only
could be the upshot, so they found Hanuman
and his army.

Hanuman's sapped groaning
two-day leave-me-alone arms-
about-the-head shush hangover
army . . .

Chapter Ten: Calling All Monkeys Here Now Please!

Sugreeva summons a monkey army.

~

The fighting season was at them.
King Sugreeva gave sober notice for a great army thus . . .

'Now all hear this, yo!
Go forth my clarion-calling monkeys,
go forth you who leap and in leaping sip the clouds!
You who simply blot the sky at full span!
You who are built like elephants and buffaloes!
You, my boldest monkeys
leave no cave, mountain or bunker in the ocean unchecked!
Go forth bringing bounding out the million billion monkeys
        lapping the global mantle
by plying them with standard inducements and gifts
and telling them there is a king of the monkeys
who calls them raging forth for the celestial battle!

Let the world reckon in millennia to come

that once in Kiskinda
King Sugreeva stood before a prophecy of monkey power
fulfilling! Where a mission to save the earth entire
was consummated and monkeys were freed ever after!
Summon them all by the tenth day from now.
Go! Go hooting forth at once my beloved ochre couriers!'

Now all should check the speech riposte, yeah.

Within ten days, monkeys spilled from forests, mountains,
caves and seas. Three hundred million monkeys,
mascara-black, came from Mount Anjana,
a thousand million who live on roots and fruits
        clamoured down from the Himalayas,
one hundred million dazzling golden monkeys down
        from the Sunset Mountains,
millions rose up from pale-peaked Mount Mandara,
millions were tawny as a lion's mane
        and stirred from Mount Kailasa,
millions were fierce as Indra and came from Vindhyas!

Flanked and ranking leaders of armies
from sun charmed land upon land,
monkeys handsome from eating only berries,
monkeys who could fly across mountain ranges,
monkeys who could morph into bears and serpents,
monkeys who could swallow a fireball
                spitting it back with missile might,
monkeys flashing tiger-teeth and diamond nails
that with tooth or nail alone could dizzy the foe,

and all the uncategorised monkeys, all the monkeys
    never named or known
    who would fight to the final limb!

Through forest and thicket the earth thickened –
where they amassed they drank up the sun,
they blotted the sun as a huge dust cloud blinkered the sky.
The ground shook to the leaps and whoops
riddling the tottered world with apocalyptic din!

Chapter Eleven: By Nala to Lanka

Rama's army seek a way for crossing into Lanka.

~

Rama pressed the Choodamani to his chest and wept,
'Sita's father gave it her on our wedding day
   and how it blazed in her hair.
Just as we throw water on the face of one
who is dying, splash words of Sita to revive me.'
Hanuman spoke beautifully. Then warned,

'I am glad to have seen Raavana –
      he is a terrifying warrior!
Even if not for Raavana, we have a fight on our hands –
Lanka will not be easy to reach or penetrate.'

He recalled Lanka's perfect four-fold protection
of water, mountain, forest and fort
as it sat on top of a mountain with a golden rampart
studded on the inside with coral and tinted beryl
but worst of all: no sailing routes for the army.

'I smashed some drawbridges,
filled up the serpent-and-shark-packed moats somewhat
and razed some of the city
but I fear all will be swiftly healed unless we can hurry.'

No one said a word in return.
Rama and his army walked south till they reached the ocean.
They gawped at the measureless waters
    snapping with serpents
that were buoyed by smelling such vivid meat.

The ocean, underworlded with mountain ranges
and vicious peaks.
At night, Ocean's violent snarling at the moon.
    Water was like sky and sky like water.
How to separate the two in the blue-grey blur . . .
    Water idly crashing out sparks
    with a noise like drums on a battlefield.

Rama felt useless before the wild
till, after prolonged staring, he became so inflamed,
he called at the ocean
whilst preparing his mighty Brahmastra arrow,
      'If you refuse to clear a path
      I will drain your channels dry.
If I pull this arrow you cannot save your teeming creatures.'

The sky shuddered and the deep waters churned upwards.
The waters stood up like a wall from the bed to the sky
    and faced the shore!

The wind bounced back off the wall and blew back many a
soldier.
The ocean wall was the Ocean-God, Varuna, who spoke thus,

'Rama,
Air, Earth, Space, Fire and Light pursue the ancient laws as
they were ordained. I too am beholden to Nature's laws. How
can I depart from my deep and wave-crammed ways? I would
offend the creator if I ceased from my duty. Yet there is one
amongst you who is cursed or blessed in that whatever he
throws onto water will not sink but will float. He alone can
subdue me. Only for him I can relent my waves, only for him
can I relent the serpents herein for your safe passage to and fro
Lanka.'

With that, Ocean went back to its splashy violent charge.

All looked around for the ONE.
Came forward from the millions monkeys
one from a remote south-eastern world, almost whispering,
'Sorry please sirs, I am Nala.
'Tis most true I inherited a problem skill.
I would throw stones as a child
and bobbling on water they would stay
not ever a one would ever sink.
If my stones bobble perchance I may bobble a bridge?'

Asked Sugreeva, 'What is it you know
about making bridges and whatnot?
'But sir I am naturally boon'd with construction skills.

My brain, my fingers and all my parts
                'tis geared to such perfection.
                I am sorry I never before thought
it worth a mention.

        And I never before been inquired after.'

Nala bowed before Sugreeva and Rama.
His chubby cheeks blushing at his own forwardness.

Nala was soon advising a thousand monkeys
        to smash mountain peaks.
Whilst some animals made stakes and lines and measuring
rods,
Nala lay each rock and stone he was passed
                                upon the ocean.
Over the rocks a roadbed of poles was placed.

When they heard of the bridge-building,
it's said the red squirrel tribes wet their fur in the surf
then rolled in the sand, then quickly ran onto Nala's bridge
and shook themselves – filling all the tiny spaces
to make the bridge firm for the 100 yojanas to touchdown!

The completed bridge was straight as a lady's hair-parting.
Nala returned to base and instructed,
'Sirs, I am certain the ether is crammed with demons.
        One power is mine to secure us.
Pleaseth you if we all formation as a dragon
then in safety will we cross with weapons and all.'

So it was the army organised themselves, with shady parasols,
banners and wave upon wave of arrows, into dragon parts.

    Nala led troops at the dragon's head,

    Sugreeva led those of the upper lip,

    Lakshmana those of the lower lip,

Chompoopan led troops comprising the dragon's crest,

Komut and Soraram led those comprising the left and the
right eye,

    Onkot commanded the body of the dragon,

    Jambavan led the two front legs,

    Tawipat led the hind legs,

    Kesorn commanded the tongue,

several million monkeys became the scales, teeth and talons

    and Hanuman tipped the tail.

Frustrated serpents gawped with their muzzled chops
whilst a prandial heads-down dragon
yomped as one

    on the bobbing causeway.

Book Fifth: Attack of the Astras Mega-Fantastic to the Death!

~

Chapter One: Panurat Dream Gardens

Rama and his army arrive in dreamy Lanka.

∼

B reaking out of the dragon in Lanka
Rama and his army landed on a perfect lawn with broad
exact paths. The trees suspended with showcase
fruits that did not fall but stood there ripe, enticing.

Heavenly Lanka with a calm polleny breeze
    where the army fed on fruit
        then dropped, on the shiny grass, asleep.

Rama sensed a worrisome perfection
and sent Hanuman to delve.
        Shrinking
        to a pip size
        he dived
        through
        and about
        the warm earth.

Once in the deep, he heard a raggedy breathing,
and as he pelted under the garden borders
he noticed the whole park
        with its perfect trees and luscious grass
        was decked upon the back of a beast.
        A beast lying deep, deep under the park.

A beast with tentacles spiralling between the roots in the soil.
Unbeknown to Hanuman, it was the narrow-eyed
serpent, Panurat. Panurat being another in the long line
of monsters happy serving Raavana,
happy to consume all unwanted visitors . . .

Panurat who was always happy to have a whole
        army upon his back
before flipping over to crush it
        into his poison soups!

Panurat heard Hanuman crammed-in in front of his face
but before seeking to up-end the army
        and feast on his mortal feed
he opened his mouth to swallow Hanuman.

Hanuman dinkily obliged but flewwwwwwwwwwwwwwwww

                into Panurat's spiky

mouth
so fast that he

> pierced out,
> in and out,
> of his brains

thus killing that mute monster ever so quietly.

Hanuman, soaked in Panurat's poisonous brain slime,
feared death
> but then remembered his own
> immortal state, that only he
> can choose the manner of his own dying.

And dying in the heady slimes of a monster
> did not seem top of his Death Wish list.

So he bathed in a lake
and watched the paradise garden
become sere and sink slowly back to sand

beneath each shuteye army head.

Chapter Two: The Dooshman Within

Raavana's brother seeks to join forces with Rama.

~

What other dangers lurked in Lanka?
No sooner were the army awake
and away for the capital
when
coming their way – was that
Raavana's brother, Vibishana?

Vibishana, it was,
seeking alliance with Rama.

Lakshmana was delighted,
'He will be a useful tool in our hand
to break open
the citadel.'

Many stared around at each other
to gauge a response at this apparent defection.
Sugreeva stared at Vibishana and said,

'What is a dooshman, an enemy, if not this, yo?

When a brother is ditching a brother,
in the midst of muddied calamity, can we defend him?

Who else might he back-stabbingly abandon
        so his means win?'

Sugreeva's nephew, Angada, looked up and said,
'At least let's watch his conduct closely, hey.'

Said Jambavan, the bear king,
        'Villainy if he hides it
        what test will spy its crouching shadow?'

This Vibishana loyalty issue caused a well-phrased debate.
Then finally, Rama stared at all and opened his heart,

'Who is not born of family? Whether it be the family
of the mother and onward to the families
        of the inquiring imagining mind
and the widest world
        where we earn our bread and our last breath . . .

Who is not ever subject
to all that lives? Would we ever desist hearing
all that lives around us is eternally speaking, is calling us

        home?

Is there a head of such a home, such a rooted family? Surely
no man alone is mighty? And if there is mighty
 then there must be mightier and even mightier
  and onward goes the universal ascent.

Should I ever seek to live on high and refuse a hand?

Would it not be a turning away from my family?
From the world? Even if I am defeated
because I have been taken in
by this man's word

I feel blissed

to have lived justly.
Could I reject whoever, however flawed,
especially if he comes bravely before me, seeking a friend?

I tell you, were Raavana seeking sanctuary
I would forgive him everything
 so why would I shame his brother?

 This is the law of my life.

Let us treat Vibishana as king-in-waiting.'

Lakshmana, from his brother's shade, walked forth,
saying, 'Is this a wonder?
 Truly Rama, you are the miracle.'

Vibishana looked down at Rama's feet
as though they had lightened his burdens,
'Believe me, my purpose was about
seeking your grace and not Lanka's kingdom.
Lord Rama, if you are conferring it, before all
        I am accepting.'

The leaders of the army consulted Vibishana
and then refined their strategy.

Once more, Rama spoke
calmly again, 'I implore all monkeys
to desist from magic, from changing into human, snake, ogre
or any other skin. I beg you, rage with the tide
        firming your own clean flesh.

We are here to fight the good fight
so long as it is just, so long as we are clean,
so long as we wipe out the dooshman within ourselves,
        there is no shame in defeat.
Only if we are true can we truly win.

Look around the borders of Lanka, when order is lost
chaos is come. Cows are giving birth to asses,
mongooses are rearing rats, cats are mating with leopards
and squabblesome mynah are flying into houses screaming

   viki-kooki, viki-kooki, viki-kooki.

But putting laughter aside, today when we fight
it is not for Sita
who lies captive behind those towers, gates and barbicans,
nor is it you fight for me, nor is it for God.

Comes the time when each heart must be emptied
of desire, must be hungry for sacrifice.
One who serves an ideal will find eternal reward.
 In sacrifice, in servitude,
 in inner silence and in doing
 we serve the ideal being,
the ideal being that harbours in ourselves –

somewhere in here

– albeit lost yet lodged in.

I say we fight for the spiritual battle raging in our souls.
I say we fight ramifying our powers of virtue
 thus we become our own bowered path
 seeking the immortal lane.'

Chapter Three: Haalaahaalaa!

The battle begins.

~

S heer routes rose up to the palace.
Rama and Lakshmana went to the northern gate
for this was where Raavana was positioned.
Hanuman went towards the western gate with the bears.
Elsewhere went Sugreeva and the fiercest monkeys.

Raksassy being nocturnal revellers
they would struggle for a morning grapple
so at the sun's zenith, in the dry winds,
Rama heralded showdown's pageantry –
the earth-shaking din of conches and drums.

But then, Rama, being ever sober
and ever the stickler for correct procedure,
knew that prior to battle the enemy should be offered
    a final stab at peace.

Sugreeva sent his own nephew, Angada,

to Raavana's palace. He flew there and was taken
to the Great Hall where Raavana stood with his ministers.

Angada had Bali's, his dad's, coiled anger.
In other words, Angada got aggro!
In other words, Angada cruising to be bruising!
So perhaps his peace-offerings to Raavana
lacked creamy cadence. In any case, the diplomacy
    was soon strained . . .

Raavana, '. . . you serve a mere man.'
Angada, 'Rama a mere man? Then Love-God's a mere archer,
Ganga a threadbare stream, heaven's nectar
stinky juice, the great Garuda mere feathers —' **'Shutting it!**
    I am a hero, boy!
Kill this effrontery messenger.'

Angada, although attacked by two raksassy,
was tickled pink to be the first on show!
He slung each raksassy under an arm
then flew them scot-free upwards before freeing them
    to fall blood-and-guts
    slap on the marble slabs.
First blood on the death-toll war board for Rama.

On the palace borders the battlefield
    where rival now clearly heard rival
and watched the dandy war-kit of garlands, leg-rings
and jangling sparkler ornaments.

Attack of the Astras Mega-Fantastic to the Death!

Loudest were those chivvied by their preferred war-drink:
    poppy heads with thickened milk
        or infusion of mohua flowers
or fermented porridge of rag known as londaa. Yaaah!

Peace snuffed, each rival
four-division army of infantry and cavalry
came forth drawn by dogs, foxes, pigs, yalis,
donkeys, buffaloes and overhead from all directions
and encircling the world
                flocks of vultures.

So many creatures partitioning the amorous gaze
between the boyish sky
        and the girly green
        meadows of Lanka.

The scene so black it could have made white-looking
that deadliest poison, deadliest for it was a by-product
churned by the gods, known as
            haalaahaalaa!

The broad-field armies were catching at the fringes,
at the thick and from overhead as they swarmed
like the unvanquishable sway of Ocean-God,
with their legs and wings bursting at the speed of Wind-God,
enough to say, the two armies fell in
like Death-God!

All roared

Yaaaaaaaaaaah!

Or roared
Huzzaaaaaaaaah!

Above all
haaalaaahaaalaaaaaaaaaaaaa
|||||||||||||||||||||||||||||||||||||||||
:::

Raksassy arrows hungering downhill
    were plugged
by bear and monkey tree-trunks chucked uphill.

Rama's army pierced through flanks
                and leapt or flew over
the shark-and-serpent infested ice-water moat of the palace.
Rampart-stationed raksassy
lunged at the beast coming over the wall.

At the palace or on the battlegrounds,
    awesome duel overtime.
As befitting our oriental monkeys

the sound of fighting with clubs
was continuous as the rhythm of footsteps:

tat-thai/tat-thai/tat-thai/tat-thai/tat-thai/tat-thai . . .

Each raksassy repeatedly swinging his
     barbed stabbing spear,
     his valayam discus,
     his trident or scimitar
that met a blocking-it-with-a-rock bear or monkey
and on they would fight until they fell to fists alone.

Then both so wounded – one would wither
and in withering fill his match with hope.

Blood and   tufts of hair   were pulled   in the final
wrench

     as   body tore   neck to neck   at body

for   desperate   tooth-and-nail   life.

In each incredible duel: hero versus hero.
Tragic personal outcome only
     for he, whose body so heckled, died fighting
          till his fatal
               final exit
                    mood-swinging
mother-summoning

265

breath! For Death'd been knocking at the door
and already gone!

Like the battle between the gods and arsooras in the olden days
the earth was soon slithery, blooded
by every earthly creature.
Weapons lay in heaps like flower offerings.
So many bodies fell by the wayside
                    and ran down the river log-like.

Both sides were feeling smoked.
Guttural, chesty reverberant roars darkened the scene

    then there were only screams

      weeping

    weird

      joy-hootings . . .

Chapter Four: Enter the Vital Invisible

Raavana's son, Indrajit, fights with Rama.

~

A nd so on raged the battle.
Rama's army soon found
they had the upper hand
    till Raavana sent his son
    Indrajit into the fray.

Indrajit could be here and not here.
    Invincible Indrajit could become
        literally invisible!

    When he was invisible
    he was a daddy's boy
        riot-act!

circular chariot. Indrajit killed from the panther-skin seat of his

Indrajit fired his Nakabat arrow
that freely knocked about the field:
one arrow dividing into many and those arrows dividing again:
from one Nakabat a thousand or so mini-Nakabat
    ballistic spears whooped

    in a deadly dreadnought insouciance!

Of the millions monkeys back for battle next morning,
Invisible Indrajit was a Death-God darkening the fields.
His panther chariot was like the wind off a monsoon.
Only his twanging was distinct. No

    movement pattern to his skedaddle

amuck-running twang.

    Rama's army was a doomsday dance.

When Indrajit had his monkey-fill,
he became the glory seeker. He went after Rama.

Invisible Indrajit
fired spears at him!

Rama looked about feckless.

Rama was: who is firing the arrows?

From where?

His dense muscle defence breached –
he was speared willy-nilly.

Then Indrajit shot spears into his

vitals, literally, into his

groins!!!

Whilst Rama lay dying, Indrajit unleashed serpent darts.
Serpents nuzzled into Rama's flesh.
Bloodsucker serpents mean you're out for the count!

Who wouldn't be out for the count?

No wonder Raavana's army went back to the palace.
Raavana could be heard partying. Indrajit stole away
and prayed to the gods.

Meanwhile, Sugreeva and Vibishana steadied the troops

as rumour of Rama's death startled each ear-to-ear.

Somehow, miraculous Rama awoke!
Rose; with barely enough focus.
    The serpents were still at him.
    He summoned a mantra.

    A mantra calling for Garuda.
That mighty eagle and drat nemesis to all serpents
    because he dines on serpents.

    Garuda leapt on Rama's mantra.

    Garuda sailing through the lands
then swooping down to beat daintily his beak and fork-claws
        at the serpents.

With impeccable dining manners he left a clean plate
and was gone.

        Go Garuda!

Chapter Five: Feel my Shakti, boy!

Raavana fights Lakshmana. Hanuman is sent to find a leaf.

~

Each morning Rama's army awoke full-sighting
Raavana's palace high up as ever on its thousand pillars
and bathing its indestructible peaking whites in the first sun.
Replenished braggart block-work egging Rama on!

And Raavana, on day three, sniffing glory,
summoned his chariot and pronto
at the door could be seen – greased gem caps
and eight gleaming horses with charioteer.

From his heavily guarded gate, Raavana went to the field.
Even though his spies informed him that Rama had survived
he posed from his chariot. If son could give Rama
a good licking, with his ten heads in every direction

he would   killlllllllllllllllllllll

them all, all by himself!

He was pure war glamour. Poster boy.
Heart-throb soft-focus-shot!

If only the girls could see him now:
could sniff his sandalwood.

Even Rama could only say,
'Raavana is the vision majestic.'

In plain view
Raavana picked up and chucked a rock –
a rock as heavy as a cloud
that's made of a comet!

His rock silenced a flank of monkeys and bears
that had been roaring towards him!

Sugreeva pulled back the army

as Lakshmana jumped in, 'Come and fight me
O mighty King!'

Raavana twanged his bow
and the enormous notes announced he was ready to fight.
Lakshmana twanged his bow.
Then both fell in.

Attack of the Astras Mega-Fantastic to the Death!

It was a battle of wondrous arrows.
Lakshmana repelling Raavana's arrows.
Raavana's arrows slit like snakes with severed bodies
so they could not fly back to Raavana's quiver.

Some fine Lakshmana shooting, or what?

Said Raavana, as they paused to reload,
'You have been a worthy warrior
    but you must go now to Yama.
This arrow was made by my father-in-law, Maya,
for me only. Feel my Shakti, boy!'

The Shakti-arrow which had seemed to come from nowhere
    save for its eight tolling bells
    was already in

    Lakshmana's chest.
Raavana knew Lakshmana was finished
    when he watched
this image of his own mighty son, Indrajit,
drop to the ground
lifeless.

Hanuman charged to the centre
    hauling off Lakshmana's body
whilst a thousand black monkeys distracted Raavana.

Poison from the Shakti could not be reversed.
    Lakshmana must die.

Rama, shocked, openly wept,

'What worth saving dear Sita
if my brother lies dying? If Sita is my heart,
brother you are my mind! Where, searching the world,
would I find another Lakshmana?

You, whose two hands have powered more arrows
    than thousand-handed
    Kaartaveeryaarjoona.

    O lift up your arms again . . .'

Rama left rubbing his brother's feet.

Jambavan, the wise bear-king, went to Hanuman,
'Hasty for the mountains go,
between Kailasa and Rishabh, in the Himalayas,
is the medicine mountain. From there pluck
the sacred plant called Visalya.
    Lakshmana might be saved by it.'

Hanuman, this son of Wind-God, was a natural carrier,
    and knew he'd need to be
    back in a jiffy to save the day.
He swung his tail till he was outstandingly expanded
then he charged for the distant mountains.

Attack of the Astras Mega-Fantastic to the Death!

Hanuman flew at the speed of Garuda
and was there plenty quick.
He saw the mountain peak.

But it had a killer discus
whirling speedily
about it

protecting the whole peak.
Besides, Hanuman's head was chocked
with the scent
of a billion balmy-breeze teeming herbs sprigging there.

He prayed for the first ever time to his
element father, that father recall son,
that father make the discus cease.

And at once, the zooming discus

came to slowly whirl and slowly
came to rest upon the peak.

Hanuman took deep breaths for he knew
his father, from however afar, was wings for him.

Hanuman shambled about the peak
trying to pluck a sprig
but each time he went to lift the sprig

the sprig

                    seemed to rescind
                    itself back into
                              stone
           from where it grew against the course of nature.

Then at once, all sprigs vanished.

A bare mountain faced Hanuman. Lakshmana will die!
           Hanuman was truly narked now.
           With his cheek-puffing might
           and thunderous muscles

                    he lifted
                    he lifted

                    the whole darn
                    mountain-crest!

The whole darn mountain-crest on a bare palm
which he flew along a wind stream

                    back to the battlefield.

           The two startled armies
           pulled back their wield and watched

as Hanuman rested the mountain.

           Then he lifted Jambavan atop
           for a gentle bear mantra.

Soon as Jambavan crooned his single note yodel

one
tee
ny

l
e
a
f

      between rocks gently peeped out its head.

The teeny peepy leaf

was lit like a lotus and beamed upwards
           for those refined
           biscuity paw-tips.

Jambavan brought the leaf before Lakshmana's
nose. The delicate, vulnerable Visalya –

      light as a curl of air

and transparent save for a whiff of green
had enough guts to yank back from the deep pit
      nigh-death
      flesh
      bounding

upwards and alive!

Lakshmana was given ample shakti
when his wounds healed and his blood plugged dynamic.

Chapter Six: Patronisation for cocky shot

Rama fights Raavana.

~

The army tried to pull Rama back
but he was riled. He stepped forth for Raavana.
How he must have felt a loathing
    for this vile wife snatcher.
A snatcher who left the husband in a conundrum
about how to win back his wife
    and have her
    as she was
    before she was taken . . .

Rama looked strained by raw mortal heat
as though a blood tongue-taste staked him useless.

    Raavana was frisky for war.
He went about the sky showboating in his chariot

        his long loose hair
        crackled electric thunder

and fiery sparks

       streamed downwind from his arms.

Rama seemed to calm, and said to his chariot-driver,
'Raavana is excited.
Let him perform his dandy antics and tire himself.
He is trying to ruffle us. Remain sure.'

       Then finally,
       face to face:
       Rama and Raavana.

Raavana was still admiring the battlefield
whilst he twanged his bow like a stringed barrel
raised high in the air in a cocky-boy style.

Rama held his bow level then twanged to begin battle.
             Their notes rose
             to heaven
             becoming
             a single
             mingling note.

      The gods swooning to the marriaged music.

Straightaway the two bow-twangers banged out arrows!
They fought so speedy it was sparks and fire.

280

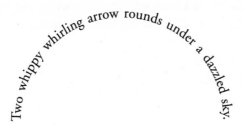

Two whippy whirling arrow rounds under a dazzled sky.

Both heroes swept their bows back into circles
with each round.
Anything with less than sporting discipline
would be repelled!

Their full-tilt energy combined
was unfelt on earth before
and jolted the moon
causing banks to break and rivers to flood.

The sea skated upwards and sliced the clouds.

The battle outcome:
Raavana, too busy, dreaming of killing
this saviour of the heavens
found that

this saviour had loaded an arrow
into his chest!

The arrow had shocked Raavana back into reality
in such a startling way

that his crowns had puttered from his heads!
His bow had popped out of his two main hands.

    Bare-headed.
    Bare-handed.
    Indigent.

    Holy war!

Rama's army was roaring! Roaring that now was the time
    to kill this effing fiend!
Kill him, Rama! Kill him now, Rama!

Rama lowered his bow and arrows, saying calmly,
'Shabash, Lord Raavana.
    You have been a wonder today.
    Truly, you have earned your kill.
You must be exhausted from your exhilarations.

Come back when you have bathed in healing salts.
    I seek combat only at your peak.'

For the first time in his thousands years
Raavana felt that gut-burbling feeling of bhaya, fear,
when he was ridden home paupered by a brawl.

Chapter Seven: Wakey Wakey Din-Din Time!

*The giant Koombarkana would do anything for his brother,
Raavana . . .*

~

Vibishana wondered to Rama,
  'I'm surprised not yet to see my brother, Koombarkana,
   called to arms.'

Said Rama, 'He is the mightiest, no?'

'In battle he has been unbeatable.
       We call him our Oooloo Ballong,
       our champion warrior!

The raksassy lords owe their might to this or that boon
       but Koombarkana's might is all his own.

From birth he was constant bulking muscly
       so he constant needed nourishing.
As a child he was a gormless gaping maw
that would scoff banquet-loads for breakfast

then still feeling famished
    he would sneakily
    swallow arsooras or even raksassy!
    Raw!

Chief raksassy went to heaven for support.
To shorten a long story,
Brahma saved the day by putting Koombarkana to sleep.
    Permanent coma.
No other way was in his locker
    to tighten the boy's appetite.
But after some parental pleading,
Koombarkana was granted wake-up time
for one whole day every six months.
That day is nigh. He dotes on Raavana.'

'Bring out the Oooloo Ballong!

Monkeys on the field need scoffing!'
said red-faced Raavana, once back at the palace.

It was a task making Koombarkana yawn
for the six months of his sleep had not ended yet.
A small army blored trumpets and whacked drums
and pulled that dire Oooloo's hair.
    Food hall was bubbling juicy vats
    with creamy kidneys, hearts and limbs
    from God knows whatever beast.

Koombarkana would be wolfing from the pillow:
he'd make a meal

of whoever he could grab when he stirred,
so it was best to have food steaming.
No more casualties during war needed!

Still asleep, elephants were ridden over his tummy.
Tickled by this, Koombarkana finally roused.
Loudest trumpets now performed most cacophonic
    to bring him home
        from the land of nod.

Koombarkana finally yawned and whilst yawning
    he popped with greedy speed
    a handful trumpet-wallahs in his gob!

Burping and rousing to consciousness
    he slobbered on corpulent gobfuls of meat
    and quaffed war-wine gallons.
He farted till the palace air was unpalatable.

Advisers filled him in about a somewhat major rumpus.
Temporarily sated
Koombarkana was then hugged by his dearly Raavana.
'Rama has our measure. He is with too many monkeys.'

Koombarkana, that proper fellow,
    showed how he could stir-in the serious
    whilst making light of the most knotted drag,

'Beloved brother, I am eaten up by your gloom.
But shouldn't a king adopt lean counsellors?

Any jabbering adviser who says wrong conduct
  is correct, I say feed him to the dogs!

Listen hard, Raavana: you should have spies chewing
on every word of your foe. If you guard your ground
  how can power go plump belly up!?

War is the final fatal morsel to be chewed on
by noble kings when all arguments are famished.

You began the last course, passing on the starter!
Did any adviser wake you from your craving,
  your rushing on another's man's dessert?
If one did, what did you consume?

But fret not your brows.
  I love snacking on live meat.
  You rest, Raav-ji, I will go for a solo paseo
  and on the way I may just fetch my own din-din!'

Then rolling up his jolly giant sleeves
and expanding in size at the thought of food from battle
  that Oooloo Ballong was

FOUR-HUNDRED BOW-LENGTHS TALL AND JUST AS WIDE.

Down the slope he thud-dud-dud-dud-duddered
but seeing the millions monkeys still active
he snacked a dream

where he was a double-roti din-din for Death.
Yet for his Raav-ji he would happy go down dining.

Straight off, his big *blam!smash!* palms
grabbed any amount monkeys then down his chompy gob
they juiced, like puréed ants!
Like ants, monkeys clambered
all over him. Any got grabbed got noshed.

And bones

like pips

were spat out

becoming clubs bludgeoning the monkeys.

Club Havoc in Club Koombarkana!

At best, the monkeys stabbed the giant with pointed
trees, firing stones at his face.
But all was pinged out and pinged back
so the monkeys lay punch-drunk or dead.

Koombarkana went after their king
but Sugreeva flew upwards, saying,

'You can brag fame now
by killing so many of my army.
Let us ruck so you can check an Oooloo foe, ho!'

Said Koombarkana, 'Brahma is your ancestor.
   Why brag?

   Show me your candy!'

Sweet flying Sugreeva whirled a rock cone
   whipped fresh from a mountain crest.
   It cycloned for Koombarkana's head!

But Koombarkana thrashed his arms about
grinding mountain-matter to a dusty phenomena

            that
          simoomed
        for the ocean.

At the receiving end of Sugreeva's whizzing about
   and rock chucking
the giant finally zoomed in on Sugreeva's movements:

   his finger-flick beserked Sugreeva

     from his spinwhizz

and sent him spiralling
downward.

Koombarkana shoved Sugreeva under his arm
and waved the other arm in victory, *yaaah!*
King as hostage would weaken monkey morale.

Attack of the Astras Mega-Fantastic to the Death!

But who fears most
        the thing in the thick of their grip . . . ?
Who doesn't become like the ape
    that the higher he climbs in the world
the more he shows his arse!?

O sloppy-cocky Koombarkana! Look under your arm
on your way back to the palace!
    Sugreeva has roused from near-death
    and is about to make his sharp attack.

Before even the Oooloo noticed,
with crystal-pointed teeth and nails
Sugreeva bit and clawed at the bulbous ears and nose.
    Near scrambling them off.

    Poor Koombarkana was dizzied.
    His small army was trounced

and he was all on his lonesome

    save for the monkeys now furring him . . .

    Rama blasted his sharpest arrows,
    they fell away
    but for the one that he had sunk in Bali.
    It took a dozen such arrows for the end-result.
A dozen such arrows before those giant arms were slit,
were discommoded

limb to limb
plop to the ground like puddings!

Queasy Koombarkana
kicked about and head-butted

biting

at anything by his chomp-yard.

Finally though
Rama shot a flank of tight-knit blade-like arrows at his neck,
so many arrows they beheaded
that bullied bugger!
Oooloo Ballong bombastic bum-up thud.
Then permanent sleep.
Then grand hoots bore at the blood-bloated hills.

Chapter Eight: The Dream Arrow

Indrajit is encouraged to be visible when fighting. The citizens of Lanka mourn.

~

I

Overnight, Sugreeva had sent an army
with firebrands to set alight towers and mansions
and smoke issued in the morning. Rama's army
had the upper hand. On the fourth morning
Vibishana had leapt from sleep, and seeing Lakshmana,

'I have been remiss for I have been forgetting
that my nephew, Indrajit, has the power to summon prayers
that will harden his body so he is free from injury
eternally. He will be able to grant his soldiers immortality.

He can achieve all this only in battle.
We must go to him. I know where he prays.'

They crept behind a hill

then stole behind a banyan tree.
Indeed it seemed Indrajit was in full spiritual flow.

Indrajit fed his altar with butter from a ladle of black iron
and rubbed marks with ashes on his brow.

Whispered Vibishana to Lakshmana,
'These marks will grant him invisibility for long enough.'

They watched cracks
    in the ground broaden and from the underworld
Naga serpents whirled forth to bathe Indrajit's javelins
    with their karella-flavoured venom.
Nearby a black goat at a stake
    which Indrajit bled for new blood.
Indrajit was then about to use the blood in an offering
    that might be making him immort –

when, 'What coward seeks personal reward in battle?
    What coward fights invisible?
Come and fight me face to face and show the gods
    you are deserving immortality,'
roared Lakshmana from behind the tree.

Indrajit, who saw his uncle step out, cajoled him,
'How can a raksassy betray his own blood?
In times and times to come, dear uncle,
I envision you fleshed
in stone or ink as a traitor, or, as we say, a pandy!'

'Have I not been serving dharma only? As one serving dharma
 you too must regard the pandy truly as the hero.'

'My dharma is to support my father, your brother!
 Is there any greater loyalty?'

Vibishana spoke firmly, 'When two factions
 are not equally clean
how can we be leaving behind what is a stain on Truth?

'Despite brotherly affection securing your safe release
from Lanka, you return having judged your brother.
Now this Rama, your new star
blazes all in his path

so Yama erase the ghost of his parting . . .

 Even a sun when it cools leaves a blot.
 What blot can ever be cleansed

 from Sita, from Rama?'

Vibishana was inwardly torn
 to see his nephew perilously visible.
But he could not kill him himself.

Lakshmana called out *coward!* again.
Indrajit had never before been, who dare do it,
 called a coward!
Indrajit was on his chariot and said,

'Lakshmana, if you have missed seeing my power before,
I pray you see it now. I ask for the gift of single combat.'
'I give it.'

Both boys twanged their bows then fought.

> They would fight for hours.
> Neither backing down.

The boys were near deaf and blind with focus.
Lakshmana admired Indrajit's speed and stamina.
> The stalemate needed unlocking,
> Lakshmana stepped up a level
and from his celestial gear he fired a missile
presided over by the Water-God, Varuna.
> Indrajit saw the missile
> looping towards him
and fired back his celestial missile
presided over by Havoc-God, Rudra.

> Rudra annulled Varuna.

And on they went till it must be curtains for one:
Indrajit plucked an arrow given him by Yama.
Lakshmana recognised it. He matched it
with an arrow given to Kubera in a dream:
> it was invincible, it was invisible!
It swallowed Indrajit's javelins as they were fired.

And forwards it continued till it realised its aim

in Indrajit's ever-so-wide windpipe.

Indrajit was choking
like a child who mistook the size of the stone in his mouth.

In mercy,
Lakshmana pulled out an arrow that was too hot to hold
but demanded to be the rending shaft.
Reciting a mantra,
whilst the arrow was burning his fingers,
Lakshmana shot the flame into Indrajit's heart.

Indrajit's innards were instantly barbecued.

II

Lay slain in Lanka, besides Indrajit,
lakhs upon lakhs dead bodies. Not buried yet
and become a banquet for flesh or fowl . . .

From Lanka came outdoors lakhs upon lakhs
raksassy women
some were there they lost their husband,
some were there they lost a son,
some were there they lost a brother, a cousin or uncle.
All were there feeling all now was lost.
Some blamed Soorpanaka for her Rama adoration,
some scorned Sita's charmed beauty.

They gathered at Lanka gates and huddled one another,
they locked arms and embraced in a tight circle.
They locked tight then set free one huge hush cry –
    one soft lamentation.
Their cry went unstraightforwardly ascending –
its heart-breaking tenderness vapoured
    and sheared off at the fringes

and as it ascended for the heavens it unfurled like a wilting flower.

    Then rising
    through that soft
    cry's pollen core
    Raavana's harsh
    sob that had shot
    separately from
    the highest palace
      turret

momentarily deafening space.

Chapter Nine: Attack of the Astras Mega-Fantastic to the Death!

Rama and Raavana fight again.

~

At the palace, Raavana attended a ritual bath.
His special prayers were assisted by Mandodari,
his dearest wife. She suggested,
'My Lord, if we end Sita – we end Rama . . .'
No answer. She tried distracting him,

'You have captured my heart always.
    I love our life.

I pray the omens are bad . . . O do not go
    where our son has gone.'

Raavana's master magician, Vidyujjivha,
was waiting in a chamber and finally had his meeting,

'My Lord, do you not hanker for a head or two?

A gore head of Rama . . . has been prepared . . .

The living dead-head double of this saviour . . .
perchance we show it to Sita? Would it send her

to sleep . . . Would this end Rama's halo-headed cause?

Or . . . on a platter I have garnished,
with a Choodamani, Sita's mimic head . . . Take it to
the battlefield . . . ?

       My Lord, what say you to my . . .

. . . dainty pair of beheaded . . .
                lovers?'

Vidyujjivha wore his glacial air,
his skin seemed made of glass, his cheeks
in the sunniest day looked scabbed with frost
and his words fell faintly as though heard
from the other side of a window pane, more seen than heard
and being seen merely guessed at . . .

Vidyujjivha kept his head down. Raavana, emphatic,
'You do well to ready your deceits but I am
already the victor, for another's wife lies in my grip.
And though it be my privilege, my prerogative
to expatiate my conquest upon the flesh of the defeated,
I would not.

Sita is our guest and must be honoured to the end.
No chink or junk thinking will blink me
from my fair fight to the death. Are we not ever
    in the eyes of the heavens?'

Raavana returned to his chambers and Mandodari
knew that with so many now fallen
her duty lay in helping her gentle husband
fasten his battle dress, armour, armlets and crowns.
She ensured that protective armour covered all his broad-bulk.

She silently tightened his sword-belt
then bolstered him with accoutrements:
decorative yet also protective. In his ample hands:
a special sword from Shiva, a double-edged scimitar, a mace,
an axe,
    a shield, a bow and so on.

Raavana was now on his chariot. The gods feared
his deaf mood. And feared earth's fate.
They rained blood as a harbinger
and even though Raavana saw the blood
with his twitching left eye
    he remained steadfast: do or die.

So the gods sent Rama their special chariot.
Rama watched the vehicle descend from the skies.
He was bowled over by a chariot and charioteer, who said,

'Lord Rama, my name is Matali.
We can move faster than light itself.
Lord Brahma has sent me to help you.'

The beat of war drums.
Lord of Mortals versus Lord of Raksassy.

Raavana blew his conch
and its shrill call resounded through the universe.

The battle that must bring both men to the end of the road . . .

Raavana's and Rama's chariots smashed hard.
Raavana glared up at the heavens.

Both held ground.

They took their chariots skywards
and fought above the clouds.
They conjured ample diamond-hard Maya-made missiles.
The strength of each in the bobbing and firing back redoubled.

Instead of one, Raavana now went twenty-fold with bows
for his twenty arms.

Rama's arrows

     broke no end   Raavana's arrows.

Attack of the Astras Mega-Fantastic to the Death!

The gods were
  horrified for the
     haemorrhaging
       earth.

Rama and Raavana were an inferno!

Wherever their missiles crashed
they blackened measureless green things
and scuttling or quarried squeaky or soundless
  thingybobs . . .

After circling the globe several times

  over several non-stop hours

the duelling chariots resumed fighting

    back in Lanka.
    Till eventually a breakthrough:

Rama's arrows so awesome they pierced Raavana's armour.

Raavana winced and was forced to change tactics,
  not now merely shooting arrows,
he called on the Astras, the supernatural forces,
to create weird effects. Rama could only imitate.

Raavana now stood atop a peak
and summoned from the far ends his deadliest weapon:
a trident that matched Death's kill trajectory.
It was once gifted to Raavana by the gods!
Yes, the gods, who watched a tad shame-faced.

The trident could be heard whooping through abysms
        and furthest cosmic ice-zones.
The noise was booming and the earth heating!
Rama uttered mantras
and realised one that turned the trident to dust.
The dust was thicker than a thousand mountains
and plugged the sea where it fell.

'These are but kitchen pussy-footing utensils,'
yelled Raavana, who had tools galore.
He summoned an old gift, from Shiva, called Danda.
It was a comet that could zone on its target.
        Target located:
        instant explosion.
Raavana summoned the doolally Danda . . .
The gods feared for Rama.
This could be it for boy wonder.

No chance! Rama's super-fired arrows,
        so many and so boosted,
        met mid-air the Danda:
                        full on explosion
                        blown into space!

Raavana brewed up Maya itself.
Maya created illusions that confused Rama.
Maya had apparently returned all Raavana's army.
Charging towards Rama came some shy and retiring types.

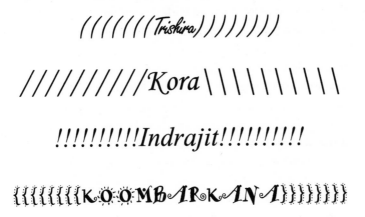

$(((((((Trishira)))))))$

$////////// Kora \backslash\backslash\backslash\backslash\backslash\backslash\backslash\backslash\backslash\backslash$

!!!!!!!!!!Indrajit!!!!!!!!!!

$\{\{\{\{\{\{\{\{ KOOMBARKANA \}\}\}\}\}\}\}\}$

Presently Rama watched all that once were belly-up
now armed
and stampeding at him.

Rama pleaded to his charioteer, Matali,
'What is happening?'
Said Matali, 'You know it not? You create all illusions.
You make dreams and dream-stuff
        such as aught from envy to poetry.

Raavana has created phantoms to foil you
whilst you are a mortal. If at all you are doubting yourself
or weakening from your mantras: Maya kills you!'

Rama sat in pure focus and sought
the Naama, or wisdom fused with perception,
a super-rare rarely, if ever, usable weapon.

Rama held firm
and not a single negative distracting thought for a blink
entered.

It was as if Rama was vanishing from flesh into
one-compacted-atom-thought.

Raavana's phantom crew was murderous breathing upon Rama
when Rama summoned Naama.

Naama instantly emptied the air of

Maya's hurtling maniacs!

Raavana was convinced his Maya would mash up Rama.
He was sickened. He thought, who is Rama?
Not Shiva, for Shiva is my ally.
He could not be Brahma, who is four-faced,
and he is not Vishnu
for I am immune generally from the holy trinity.

Perhaps he is the primordial being.
The cause behind the universe?

Death's elation would be to uncover
    the spring, the source.
        What then if I beat it?

Would I be killing myself in killing the source of creation?

Raavana went back to his mental kitchen, as it were.
He remained unfazed by Rama. Unfazed by death.
He focused again and unleashed an effect known as Thama.

Thama spun out arrows that orchestrated

    darkness everywhere.

Thamas flew out from near Raavana's body.

Each Thama had a head that spat up fangs and fiery tongues.
In no time, not a candle was lit in any nook.

But more, total darkness emptied all worlds.
All worlds! Starless end-to-end darkness.

        Creation paralysed.

Amidst the darkness

rain deluge on one side

and stone-pour on the other.

Darkness and stone pelting in absolute torrent.

Add to this torrent tornadoes sweeping

the earth with hail-storms!

All earth, all cosmos was now near kaput.

In thickest thunder, storm and darkness
                              Rama was crouched in a cave
                              praying

summoning all sorts of remarkable forces
that the greatest sages would have barely imagined imaginable.

Still Rama and the cosmos were dying.

Somehow Rama survived those rocks
that tore at his cheeks? In surviving, he somehow focused

to summon a Shivasthra.

A Shivasthra understands the general apocalyptic mania
                    thriving in a Thama

so was able to annul Thama. Annul Thama in a stroke
as though the world's end had come and gone!

Apocalypse abated and refulgence returned,
though many rare ones became extinct.

Raavana reacted with rage at this defeat.
He came down from his mountainous perch –
roaring at Rama on the battleground
by blindly emptying endless arrows at him.

Rama's arrows met Raavana's arrows halfway
        and turned them all round
so they stacked in Raavana's chest!
So they stacked in Raavana's chest.

Chapter Ten: Ample Head over Heart lacking

Rama seeks a way to kill Raavana.

~

Rama went for the death
  calmly slicing off Raavana's heads,
    one by one, hurling them into the ocean!

Rama's blade thundered as it sliced
    each dense-as-Time boon-bolstered head
    YET
soon after lopping each exhausting head

    Rama observed an exact-dense head

        sprouting back on Raavana's neck!

    Each grown-back head threw up
foul-worded dares at Rama
but Rama calmly kept at his lumberjacking.

A hundred mighty heads fallen

and a hundred were back on
till eventually Raavana weakening . . .

fainted.

Matali whispered to Rama,
'Finish him for good now. It is all over!'

But Rama panting, 'It is unfair in combat
to attack a man who has fainted. I will let him recover.

Mareecha, Kara, Indrajit and Koombarkana were killed
        but how do I end Raavana's career?'

Matali, who was the god's charioteer
and used to battles, simply said, 'Raavana will grow
heads endless. You must now use the Brahmastra.'

When Raavana was back on his feet
he took out his sword, crying at his charioteer,
'Why did you pull us away?
        The gods will think I showed fear.'

Said the tearful charioteer,
'But Lord, Rama stopped fighting.
Our horses needed shade from the sun's rays.
My life, my duty is to your kind love.'

'I am glad you serve me, would you take this?'
Raavana awarded his charioteer

a gem-encrusted bracelet given him by the gods.

With his chest already healed
Raavana lifted his many swords
    charging wildly at Rama

but Rama slapped all his swords cleanly away.

With nothing left to lose, Raavana threw
    whatever came to hand
whether it be staves, cast-iron balls or boulders.

Pleaded Matali, 'O Lord, he is becoming mighty again!
    Could he war once more?
You must try summoning the Brahmastra.'

Rama worried about using this weapon originated by Brahma.
It was only to be used in the final event.
The shaft of the arrow bore the essence of the skies.
It was heavy as Mount Meru
and contained the combined energy of all beings.

Along annihilation's path it could spray up
        mountains and oceans innumerable.

If not used correct on the battlefield
it could blank all in its path from east to west as it went.

It was Yama's role model, for sure.
It needed masterful sorcery-calling

and could only be summoned by one once in a lifetime.

> Rama was fending off
> Raavana's lumbering
> lumpen weapons

as he began his chant.
He chanted for the Brahmastra
nursing it concentratedly into its cleanest perceivable aim.

All creation sat up for a second
and Raavana's ears pricked at a whizzing spear.

A fire hearse bombing through the billion galaxies
with all their ordered and remiss back-rooms and chambers
that formed the furthest span of the universe.

Raavana knew he was hearing the Brahmastra
    clearing past the cosmic ceiling
    and already clearing the mountains
    and already booming for his heart
    and he knew he was vulnerable
    at heart
(something he had never sought protection for)

and the Brahmastra had already plunged him

into the blue

then burst him back

Attack of the Astras Mega-Fantastic to the Death!

                      colossal up towards the stars

      and the spatial doom

before he was speared back down to earth

upon the furrowed routes

        with a black gap

a black gap chasming his chest. His smithereen heart.

In all the worlds, to all the gods from distant times
it must have been implausible
a god could be razed by a mortal.
Inconceivable that Raavana could not be inviolable.

Raavana's hefty crowns and jewellery
scattered pell-mell about his black-as-collyrium body.

Chapter Eleven: Duty

Vibishana and Mandodari mourn.

~

Even in victory Lord Rama was pure
forgiveness. When Vibishana, so overwhelmed with grief,
pulled up a blade and was about to cut off his own head
Rama spoke through sighs,

'Is there a home for hatred

> after death has blown off the roof?

O bravest of all, Vibishana, your brother is now
our brother. We must honour him a funeral
> so his spirit may course
> for its place in heaven.

Will you not serve him, now?'

Vibishana was crowded with tears as he whispered,

'What might he
have achieved?'

Mandodari ran to the battlefield
and fell upon her lord's body sobbing.

Mandodari called blindly aloud,
'Is all joy now gone
and we are manacled to the millstone?

        My Lord, do you leave me
        no sign?

            In our lives to come
            how will you know me?'

Mandodari fainted deep into a dream lane.

Chapter Twelve: Let's have a Cak Party calling it Diwali!

Rama, Sita and Lakshmana return to Ayodhya.

~

Fourteen years had elapsed and Rama returned
at the spot, on the dot: Ayodhya.
He was a hero bringing home
a millennium reign of peace.

King Sugreeva, King Vibishana and Jambavan
made the long journey north to honour the king of all kings.
The journey to the palace was already lit
from every house and yard of the path with candles
and red cloth was draped from door to door along the streets.

Rama's mothers and Bharat were at the palace gates
so the golden slippers on the throne meet the lord.
Alongside them waiting was Rama's favourite elephant,
        Shatrunjaya, already prostrated.

Dancing troupes wore khon-masks
    for demons and heroes
    or wore simple cottons
and were caught in the Cak dance – the trance dance
    where a male choir hummed

    ecak-ecak-ecak-ecak-ecak

and dancers mimed the already infamous abduction of Sita
    and Rama's victory
    to which the capital cheered.

The capital overcome and ready to party, alright.
    Let's have a party calling it Diwali.

Home and at the palace gates . . . at last Rama was free,
free to act of his own accord. A king with the trappings
of power. But first,
queen would finally meet her king.

But where was Sita? And why had Rama not met her
    after victory in Lanka?

Why had Sita been flown from the battle scene to Ayodhya
    in Hanuman's chariot?

And why now, here, finally, was Sita being escorted
before the palace gates? And before Rama in public?

And at last Rama looking in Sita's direction,
    looking at her as though for the first time
        surely?

Yet Rama did not look as foot-rooted by Sita
as he had been on their first ever
encounter
when he had been struck by the vision on its balcony.

    Rama raised a hand to
    calm the jubilant gathering.

    All awaited Rama's speech.
    Rama only said,

'I want everyone to observe my reunion.

    Please, Hanuman, bring down
    Sita from her palanquin.'

                Sita blushed
                at being exposed
                in this public way.

She held at the tip of her fingers the
RAMA-inscribed wedding ring for its elated return.
Sita's fawn eyes looked at Rama's hands:
    they saw there no Choodamani.

Rama's hands pointed down to the grooved earth.
He spoke not courtly but court-like with his wife
        in full view,

'Blessings on your salvation.
Our mission has been accomplished.
You have been freed from suffering.'

'You never left my heart,
                how could I suffer, Lord?'

Rama, still not looking at Sita for it would be a looking into

        light.

He continued his judgement, 'After all this
        this residence
far from your rightful home
I must tell you, as you will know,

it is not in our custom

committing back to the marital contract

                a wife

who has been resident

elsewhere, in a stranger's home.

> I have executed
> what any man must.

I have wiped out

> dishonour's stain.'

Rama looked broken. In two.

'Everyone here has seen I do not touch

> you.

There can be no question of our

living together.

> I leave you

> > free

to go wherever you please. Look about you:
ten directions or more where you can be free.

> I grant freedom to you there.'

Sita stood thunderbolted.

The crowd stunned. Yet the lord was brave to act correct
and not appear henpecked or a fool to take back a wife
    so heavily desired by another man
        whose house she had stayed alive in.

Correct indeed, Lord.

Almost to herself, 'Why peril the earth?
Why not send word with Hanuman . . .

    Truly, I would have removed the stain I am.'

Then looking at Rama, 'He who touches my body
touches not me; I am deep in myself where you live.

My Lord, you are where you stand
    but
you are in here too, so who dare touch me?

My heart, my love, my fidelity are alone
things that only I control and they are yours always.'

Rama could not reply.

'Would you rather the earth
that gave me

take me?'

Silence.

'O my man elect: my man only.'

Sita heard herself asking Lakshmana to build a fire.
        Rama nodded agreement.

Unnerved Lakshmana
        burst out a hideous high-cracking laugh!
It was a shocker and its continuance smacked all at the sore:
a short high laugh that made each feel mocked
and drawn to their own shortcomings.

It seemed as though everyone was there
yet somehow looking away from the scene
        whilst contemplating Sita,
        the crown of the glorious war
about to immolate herself . . . End nobly her suffering
with husband the chaperone to her final breath . . .

A jewel-embedded bower was laid
        on heaped wood and coal
        so Sita had a throne.

A kingly fire raged tall soon enough
for Lakshmana was of course a fine fire-starter.

All the time Rama remained still
as though readying himself for utter peacetime.

He remembered their cottage in the forest
where once in the open he had fallen asleep on Sita's lap,
and when he had fully rested he awoke to watch
raw wounds on Sita's hands and cheeks
and Sita had said, shyly,
'Rama, a crow was nipping me
but I could not disturb you. You lay there so beauteous.'

And here he was now watching Sita, beauteous as ever,
with toenails red as rubies,
in her tattered bark-skin, calling out to Fire-God,

'O Agni, I surrender myself.'

Sita, who had lived the exile
of Lord Rama,
Rama, whose hands held eternity and a minute

in that moment

held back from the hands of a wife
                who stepped

      for her throne
        in the fire

as though she was raised to her realm on the lotus.
Liquid fire become the flooding waters
            of Time
            'neath her feet.

    And every bystander a witness.
      Immolation's accomplice
      before the lord's will.

So it is with the vessel, the bark of our being,
which in the very act of its separation
    from its own flesh, own breath,

    in the final air of its parting

    it hearkens blindly after itself,
    after just its name even

    but cannot retrieve the sound
    but cannot retrieve
           the
              sound . . .
  So it was

  in that split
Sita's yarn was virtually spun.

Epilogue: Prayer

Agni and Brahma visit Earth.

~

A gni could brook no more.
Agni breaking through

      into the fire.

   Agni raising Sita.

      Sita dripping in gold.
      A golden doll.
      Her head dropped
      as one who has been
         dipped in

shame.

Said Agni, 'Lord Rama, if gold has been lost in mire
in mire it will glow for its beholder.

Let its essence find proof fantastic in Sita.
    Neither skin nor even a hair is bereft.
    She is yours to adore.'

Rama was astounded. And blessed Sita.

The gods were so disturbed by what they had watched
    that only unto this moment
        did Brahma

        hover towards Ayodhya.

Sereneness was suddenly everywhere sunshine and breeze:
not a slip in the loveliness of the world could be felt

when Brahma, bearded, was speaking prayer-like.

'Rama, of the trinity I am become Creation.
Shiva is Destruction and Vishnu is the Preserver.
    We three have borne all existence
from the Supreme Being. We are subject
to the waters of dissolution and the fire of birth.
        We are the range.

Though there are worlds upon worlds below
and worlds upon worlds above,
    and there in the midst

Earth, the Supreme Being alone is everywhere
    at home.

The Supreme Being is the heart.

The Supreme Being alone is timeless
and suffers neither birth nor death nor growth.
Such a one is void of beginning or end.
        Or in-between.

Such a one is only you, Rama.

Rama, you are Vishnu
    but you are more than Vishnu.

If you are not, Rama, existence is mere air.

You are the mantra, the syllable sacred.
    The unknown, the unknowable

even to yourself.

In yourself you are a billion eyes and a billion feet
    and you uphold time
    by living in all that lives.

You are everything that dies and everything that revives.
You are the element, the space and the depth entire.
You are the range. The range unbound.

Rama, you are God.

Sita is purer than light. Sita is Lakshmi.
Sita is the journey of your existence,
    the plenitude of your source.

Rama, without Sita you are mere air.

Rama and Sita, you are the twain essence of life.
You are the twain endurance of the essence.
You are the spirit. The spirit unbound.
You are the breath. The breath unbound.'

When Brahma had spoken,
the world stooped before Rama.

    Rama, weeping, saying,
    'Lord, I am only man.'

Rama by Sita side by side
unable to move or utter aught
save all now and evermore praying

Shanti!   *Shanti!*   *Shanti!*

Acknowledgements

~

I AM GRATEFUL to the following writers for their advice: Imtiaz Dharker, Rachel Dwyer, Aviva Dautch, Ushma Williams and Paula Richman and to Archana Rao, at Faber and Faber, for being a reader of my version.

I am indebted to the inspired Helen Taylor for the Thresholds Project that put me in touch with the generous staff at the Museum of Archaeology and Anthropology in Cambridge, in particular: Sarah-Jane Harknett, Mark Elliott and Sudeshna Guha (who was a reader of my version).

I am grateful to my editor, Matthew Hollis, for his belief in this project at its earliest stages. Above all my version owes a huge debt to my wife, Katherine Hoyle, for her constant love, enthusiasm and critical feedback.

The project was made possible by a Grants for the Arts award from Arts Council England, an award from The Society of Authors and from The Royal Literary Fund.

The translators of the *Ramayana* to whom I am most indebted are: William Buck, John Brockington and Mary Brockington, Michael Dutt, Romesh Chunder Dutt, Robert Goldman, Ralph T. H. Griffith, U. Thein Han, George L. Hart and Hank Heifetz, R. K. Narayan, Ray A. Olsson, Sanjay Patel, M. S. Poornalingam Pillai, Savero Pou, C. Rajagopalachari, Sachchidanand Sahai, Arshia Sattar, Kamala Subramaniam, Baljit Kaur Tulsi and Swami Venkatesananda.

Many enthusiasts and scholars developed my knowledge of the *Ramayana*. Chief amongst these were: Dewan Bahadur, Stuart H. Blackburn, Suniti Kumar Chatterji, Kathleen M. Erndl, Robert Goldman, Acharya Hemachandra, J. Kats, Anna S. King, Gauri Parimoo Krishnan, Ramdas Lamb, J. P. Losty, N. R. Navlekar, V. Raghavan, K. S. Ramaswami Sastri, V. S. Srinivasa Sastri, A. K. Ramanujan, Velcheru Narayana Rao, Paula Richman, Frank E. Reynolds, P. L. Amin Sweeney, David Shulman and Monier Williams, and mostly, John Brockington and Mary Brockington

Extracts have previously appeared in *Bengal Lights*, *London Review of Books* and *Poetry Salzburg*.

DALJIT NAGRA